South end Neighborhood Housing Initiative

SOUTH END
NEIGHBORHOOD HOUSING INITIATIVE

SENHI

CITY OF BOSTON · MASSACHUSETTS

OFFICE OF THE MAYOR
RAYMOND L. FLYNN

February 11, 1987

Chairman Robert L. Farrell
Boston Redevelopment Authority
City Hall, One City Hall Square
Boston, MA 02201

Dear Chairman Farrell:

As I stated in my communication of January 9, 1987, I believe
that the South End Neighborhood Housing Initiative (SENHI)
offers us an opportunity to increase affordable housing for
residents of the South End and the city of Boston. After careful
review of the financial analysis prepared by the Director and
the BRA staff, I have concluded that the SENHI Program must
require that 1/3 of the units be made affordable to families
with incomes at or below 50% of the SMSA median income; 1/3
at or below 80% of the SMSA median; and 1/3 at market levels.
I base this decision on a number of factors including:

°The preponderance of the comments received during
the extensive community review process support
this position;

°The need for affordable housing in the city of
Boston and in the South End in particular is
critical;

°The financial gap caused by this requirement is
manageable;

°Affordability is my top priority whenever the city
sells vacant land or buildings for housing
development.

Community Planning Standards

My position throughout the SENHI process has been that maximum
affordability cannot be achieved at the expense of other
community values. Therefore, the program must contain the
following planning standards:

°All sites must comply with existing zoning and
parking requirements (.7 parking spaces per unit);

°Parcels 30 and P-6A should remain as community
gardens and no disposition of garden sites should
be proposed until an open space plan for the South
End is undertaken;

°Historic preservation and design guidelines for
the South End must apply to all rehabilitation
and new construction.

The community's concerns about maintaining existing zoning,
design quality, parking requirements and open space needs have
production cost implications but, in my judgement, these values
are important and cannot be lost in the SENHI process.

Increase Home Ownership

The SENHI Program should also be an opportunity to increase
home ownership for first-time home buyers. Boston has one
of the lowest rates of home ownership of any city in America.
With a 30% home ownership level we are far below the national
average for cities (55%) and the national average for all
families (65%). Home ownership is the best way to give
Bostonians a share in their city and its growth economy. It
also has the effect of giving stability to neighborhoods which
find themselves in the path of growth. Accordingly, priority
should be given to proposals which maximize home ownership
opportunities. Nothing should prevent this goal from being
achieved through the use of cooperatives or other innovative
forms of equity participation.

Capacity Building

From the outset an important component of SENHI has been the
concept of capacity building. What Boston is developing is
a new generation of housing producers. The Bricklayers/Laborers
Non-Profit Development Corporation, Urban Edge, Tent City
Corporation, the Infill Collaborative, Douglass Plaza Associates,
Tenants Development Corporation, and so many others are breaking
new ground for Boston. The common thread is that community
people in partnership with the city and state are rebuilding
their neighborhoods for their neighbors. To give a further
boost to this new generation of housing producers, preference
should be given to Minority Business Enterprises, Community
Development Corporations, and joint ventures involving these
groups. Community based developers with good track records
in the South End, or with affordable housing, should be
encouraged to share their skills and capacity with the emerging
group of new producers.

Program Innovation and Partnership

To close the financial gap caused by the affordability
requirements and the community planning constraints, the program
must encourage innovation from the community development
proponents. The maximum flexibility on the use of disposition
proceeds from the sale of units and property must be explored,
with all proceeds used to close the financial gap. The city
will commit existing HOP reservations to the extent necessary
to promote opportunities for first-time home buyers. In addition
to these contributions we will need assistance from the state
to achieve the affordability goals established for this program.
The success we have realized in the past three years in producing
affordable housing despite the absence of federal funds is
due in part to the fine working relationship we have with the
Dukakis administration. With their help and the able assistance
of Representative Byron Rushing, who has contributed so much
to the SENHI process, and the support of his colleagues who
represent this neighborhood, we can achieve the affordability
goals which have been supported overwhelmingly by the community.

The special efforts the community, city and state must make
for SENHI to work underscore the significance of the federal
government's retreat from its responsibility to provide
affordable housing. The need to produce affordable housing
will not lessen, even though our resources are reduced, until
new leadership at the national level commits the resources
of the nation to the national problem of affordable housing.
Until that time, the burden falls on local leadership, public
and private, to find new ways to meet affordable housing needs.

I am confident that working together we can make SENHI a fine
addition to the new types of community partnerships that Boston
is developing. To expedite this program I would like the Request
for Proposals issued by March 2, 1987.

In conclusion, I would like to note for the record that the
South End community deserves whatever credit is due for
fashioning this affordability policy. Through many meetings
and countless hours of community debate, although many issues
were raised and differences of opinion were voiced, the central
theme from all sides was a common desire to make the South
End neighborhood a better place to live. This neighborhood
spirit is the real cornerstone of the community partnerships
emerging in Boston.

Sincerely,

Raymond L. Flynn
Mayor

SOUTH END HOUSING PRODUCTION COST MODEL

SOUTH END HOUSING PRODUCTION COST MODEL

The community has made clear its view that all new development and rehabilitation should conform to existing zoning and should provide the necessary parking, open space, and the quality of design and materials that are typical of recent development projects in the South End

The Administration's position throughout the SENHI process has been that greater affordability would not be achieved at the expense of the community -- not through inappropriate density, relaxed parking or open space requirements, or cheaper labor or materials   However, the community's planning guidelines regarding zoning, design, parking, and open space do have production cost implications   Since greater affordability can only be achieved by lowering production costs, these planning guidelines limit the field of cost factors that can be reduced to increase affordability

Numerous studies have been done to identify the costs of housing production and ways to lower them   The analysis in this report focuses on the major housing production cost components to determine how they may be adjusted to reduce the gap between total development cost and project income at desired levels of affordability

o   Land   The price a developer must pay for land is usually between 15 and 25 percent of the total development cost for a residential project   Because land is such a large component of housing production costs, lowering the price of land can significantly increase affordability.   The land in the SENHI program is publicly-owned, and can therefore be disposed of at costs well below market prices

This analysis tests the subsidy value of the city-owned land and buildings at various levels of affordability   Two land value options are employed   The first is fair reuse value (FRV)   FRV is the fair market value of the property for its highest and best uses permitted under the Urban Renewal Plan, reflecting both the advantages created by the project and the requirements and limitations on land uses to be imposed on the redeveloper by the Plan   Land is also valued at a below-market rate (BMR) that reflects a land payment for the portion of land attributed to the market units, and zero land cost for the portion of land attributed to the affordable units.

The value of the city's land and structure contribution to SENHI can be estimated using the FRV method   Assuming no affordability criteria were attached to the rehabilitated or newly-constructed units, the land would be valued in excess of $11 million   With the affordability distribution required in SENHI, a developer's expected yield from the land and buildings and therefore the price a developer would be willing to pay for them, is lower   Under the conditions required by SENHI, the estimated FRV of the city-owned land and buildings is $4 7 million

o   Financing   Financing, or the cost of money, is a cost during the construction phase of a project and at "take-out", when the housing is purchased by the ultimate owner   The interest rate on construction or permanent financing is the price a borrower must pay to borrow money   Construction loan interest is a component of the "soft cost" of produc-

-1-

tion   To the extent this interest rate is lower, so too will be the total cost of production   Permanent loan interest is what an owner must pay to purchase housing in addition to the actual cost of producing the housing   This mortgage interest must be figured into what a household can afford to pay per month for housing   To the extent that interest rates on permanent loans are lowered, the household can afford to buy or rent more housing on a given income

This analysis examines how state housing assistance programs such as MHFA tax-exempt bonds, SHARP, Chapter 707, Homeownership Opportunity Program (HOP), and CDAG, as well as federal assistance through Section 8 and HODAG can be used to lower the cost of financing

o   Transactions Costs   The developer's profit, and fees for architectural, legal, engineering, and other development-related services are a significant component of production costs   Developer's profit, for instance, often accounts for between 15 and 20 percent of total development costs This analysis looks at varying profit assumptions, depending upon whether a for-profit or non-profit entity is developer   Fee costs and other soft costs are assumed to be lower for non-profits   These costs can be brought down even lower by obtaining services on a pro bono basis or by reducing development risk

Land, financing, and transaction cost factors were tested within two developer models   Model I assumes the soft cost and profit expectations of a private, for-profit developer   Model II reflects the development cost assumptions of a non-profit or Community Development Corporation (CDC)   In both models, cost assumptions were derived from pro formas obtained from for-profit and non-profit developers of residential development projects in the South End within the past eighteen months   Basing the production cost model on current actual experience in the South End neighborhood in our judgement rests the SENHI policy on firmer ground   Abstractions based on state or national experience could grossly exaggerate, in either direction, probable production costs   A critical analysis of this model framework and underlying cost assumptions was performed by a Boston-based private economic consulting firm

The gap between the total development cost and project income was calculated for each model-cost scenario assuming one-third of the units are low-income, one-third are moderate, and one-third are market rate   For each model, the model-cost scenario with the lowest gap was tested at two additional affordability distributions   (1) 25 percent low-income units, 25 percent moderate-income units, and 50 percent market rate units, and (2) 17 5 percent low-income units, 17 5 moderate-income units, and 65 percent market rate units

Margin of Error

Normally, projects include an estimated contingency for unexpected events which have costs implications   Market experience in the South End shows a contingency range of 3 percent to 10 percent   We have chosen the higher number for rehabilitated units because unforeseen problems during the rehabilitation of vacant buildings, many of which have been abandoned for twenty years, are most likely to occur   A five percent contingency amount was selected for new construction units, for which this potential cost premium is much less likely

MODEL-COST ASSUMPTIONS

Transaction			A 33% Low 33% Moderate 33% Market	B 33% Low 33% Moderate 33% Market	C 33% Low 33% Moderate 33% Market	D 17½% Low 17½% Moderate 65% Market	E 25% Low 25% Moderate 50% Market
6% Arch/Eng; 3% Legal; .4% Acctng; 4% Developers Fee; 18% ROGS; 15% Equity	I	Land	FRV	FRV	BMR	BMR	BMR
		Subsidy	No	Yes	Yes	Yes	Yes
4% Arch/Eng; 1.5% Legal; .2% Acctng; 4% Developers Fee; 5% Equity	II	Land	FRV	FRV	BMR	BMR	BMR
		Subsidy	No	Yes	Yes	Yes	Yes

NOTES

A   Affordability Assumptions·

1)   Scenarios I(a), I(b), I(c),   1/3 units at 50% of SMSA median income;
      II(a), II(b), II(c)   1/3 units at 80% of SMSA median income;
                                      1/3 units at market rates

2)   Scenarios I(d), II(d)   17 5% at 50% SMSA of median, 17 5% at at
                                      80% of SMSA median; 65% at market rates

3)   Scenarios I(e), II(e)   25% units at 50% of SMSA median, 25% at 80%
                                      of SMSA median, 50% at market rates

B   Zoning·

The development program assumed for each site is consistent with
existing zoning, design, and historic preservation requirements of the
Boston Zoning Code, with the exception of open space requirements   All
design-related assumptions are consistent with the requirements of the
National Register of Historic Places

C.   Unit Sizes

    1)   Market rate units are assumed to be evenly divided between
         one-bedroom and two-bedroom units.   Low- and moderate-income
         units are assumed to be 2/3 two-bedroom and 1/3 three-bedroom
         units

    2)   Gross Square Foot unit sizes are assumed to be weighted averages
         of 1,004 square feet for newly constructed units and 944 square
         feet for rehabilitated units

D.   Land

    1)   FRV   Fair Reuse Value   Calculated at $25,000 per market unit for
         new construction on vacant land and $35,000 per market unit for
         the rehabilitated buildings, and $10,000 per moderate-income unit,
         and $5,000 per low-income unit for both new construction and
         rehabilitation

    2)   BMR   Below Market Rate   Land cost is paid for market rate units
         only

E   Hard Costs

Hard costs include site preparation, general conditions, landscaping,
paving, interior finish, materials, labor, insurance, bonding, contractor's overhead, and contractor's profit and are assumed at $75/GSF
for rehab and $90/BSF for new construction

F   Soft Costs

1)   For-Profit Developer: 6% Architectural/Engineering; 3% Legal,   4%
     Accounting, 4% Developers Fee, all percentages are of Hard Cost in
     all scenarios, except that equity is a percentage of Total
     Development Cost (TDC)

2)   Non-Profit Developer   4% Architectural/Engineering, 1.5% Legal;
      2% Accounting, 4% Developers Fee

3)   For-profit scenarios assume 15% return on gross sales for
     condominiums, on equity in the case of rental. Non-Profit scenarios
     assume no profit (breakeven) for condominiums, or 6 6% standard
     MHFA return on equity in the case of rental

4)   Scenario I assumes a developer equity requirement at 15% of TDC
     by the construction lender   Scenario II assumes an equity require-
     ment at 5% of TDC for sales, 10% for rental

5)   10% contingency for rehabilitation may exceed standard market
     assumptions by 2-5%, but serves as a buffer against hidden
     site-related and transaction costs. Contingency is 5% for new
     construction

6)   Construction period interest assumes a one-year construction period
     and a 50% average drawdown of the construction loan.

7)   Condominium carrying cost is for interest on construction loans from
     the time of the completion of units until the sale of units assuming
     an average 6 month sale period

8)   Rent-up expenses in the Rental scenarios are assumed at an aver-
     age of $600 per market unit and $300 per low- or moderate-income
     unit

9)   For-sale marketing expenses are assumed at an average of $600 per
     market unit and zero for low- and moderate-income units

10) $500 per unit Tregor fees for low- and moderate-income units are
     assumed to be absorbed as a development expense

G   Sales Expense, Rent-up, Marketing

1)   5% brokerage fees assumed for all market units in all scenarios

2)   In the Non-Profit scenarios the developers fee and 2% sales ex-
     penses are assumed to be adequate to fund non-profit operations
     for the processing of applications for low- and moderate-income
     units

H   End Loans

1) Scenarios I(a), and II(a), assume conventional permanent financing
    terms   All other scenarios assume MHFA Homeownership Opportunity
    Program (HOP) terms for permanent financing, 5 5% fixed 30 year
    MHFA mortgage loans for low- and moderate-income units   5% down
    payment assumed to be required for all low- and moderate-income
    units

2) Low- and moderate-income sales prices are derived from the house-
    hold's ability to pay, assuming that 20% of the household income is
    allocated to pay mortgage principal and interest   Other costs
    including (1) mortgage insurance (at 0034 times mortgage amount),
    (2) property insurance (at 0075 of unit cost), (3) property taxes
    (at 80% of assessed value times .01642 minus $120), and (4) condo-
    minium (fees at $75 00 per month) should equal less than 28% of
    household income

I   Rental

1) Section 8 rents used were published by HUD on 9/1/86 and are
    assumed to include all utilities   In the absence of section 8,
    chapter 707 subsidy would be used   707 rents are lower (1 BR =
    $537; 2 BR = $629, 3 BR = $769) than section 8 rents by $30 to $70
    per month   The use of lower 707 rents in some cases is assumed to
    be offset by higher section 8 rents in other cases (where waivers
    are obtained from HUD for qualifying tenants)

2) Maximum possible SHARP allocations are assumed at $3,245 per 2 BR
    per annum and $3,895 per 3 BR per annum

3) Low- and moderate-income rent in the Tenant Income section of the
    Rental Income Standards is 50% or 80%, respectively, of SMSA
    median income times 25 divided by 12   Section 8 income is the
    HUD Fair Market Rent minus the Tenant Income

4) Total Low Income rents in the Rental Operating Pro Forma may
    appear high because (a) SHARP is allocated between low- and
    moderate-income units only and (b) the credit is considered income
    to the low-income units only

5) 5% vacancy rate is assumed for all units. Thus, gross annual
    income figures are adjusted accordingly except for SHARP and
    syndication

6) Syndication proceeds for the MHFA-financed rental scenarios are
    calculated as 4% of the Total Development Cost allocable to low-
    income units minus land, minus 30% for transaction costs, minus a
    30% discount factor   A 9% credit is used in the non-MHFA rental
    scenarios   No proceeds are available if the percentage of
    low-income units is below 20%

-6-

J. Present Value Calculations

All present value calculations are made using a mid-year convention, with the "present" defined as the start of the construction year   The discount rate, 6 9% per year, was chosen to reflect the yield of general obligation (G O) bonds for 15 years. The discounted values assume a public subsidy in the form of a stream of payments over 15 years, rather than one up-front payment

FINANCIAL ANALYSIS
SUMMARY

SUMMARY OF POTENTIAL OPTIONS

Phase	# of Units	Rental/Owner	Affordability	Sites	Developer	Gap
IA	79	79-Homeowners (79 First-time home buyer)	26 @ 50% SMSA 26 @ 80% SMSA 27 @ Market	Vacant Buildings: SE-110, SE-116, RR-121, SE-13, SE-72, SE-59-66	Competition with preference to MBEs, CDCs, and Joint Ventures with these groups	$2.6-3.8 million'
IB	252	100-Rental	33 @ 50% SMSA 33 @ 80% SMSA 34 @ Market	Vacant Parcels:** R-11C, RE-7B, 29A, R-12A, R-12B, 33B, SE-98A	Competition with preference to MBEs, CDCs, and Joint Ventures with these groups	$1.8-1.9 million'
		152-Homeowners (101 First-time home buyer)	51 @ 50% SMSA 50 @ 80% SMSA 51 @ Market		Competition with preference to MBEs, CDCs, and Joint Ventures with these groups	$5.6-8 million'
TOTALS	331	231-Homeowner (180 First-time home buyer) 100-Rental	110 @ 50% SMSA 109 @ 80% SMSA 112 @ Market		($3 million) SENHI di: position proceeds ($1 million) CDAG	$6-9.7 million

* Gap amounts in excess of city land write-down, HOP, SHARP, Section 8/Chapter 707, and tax syndication subsidies

** Parcel P-6A and Parcel 30 will be maintained as garden sites.

SALES ANALYSIS SUMMARY
REHABILITATION - 79 UNITS

Affordability		I — For-Profit Developer Sales Proceeds	- TDC	= Surplus (Gap)	II — Non-Profit Developer Sales Proceeds	- TDC	= Surplus (Gap)
1/3 at 50% SMSA median; 1/3 at 80% SMSA median; 1/3 at market	A	$ 5,760,502	$10,909,186	($5,148,684)	$ 5,760,502	$ 9,849,694	($4,089,192)
	B	$ 6,849,858	$11,094,377	($4,244,519)	$ 6,849,858	$ 9,871,481	($3,021,623)
35% afford-ability: 17½% at 50% SMSA median; 17½% at 80% SMSA median; 65% at market	C	$ 6,849,858	$10,675,094	($3,825,236)	$ 6,849,858	$ 9,449,654	($2,599,796)
50% afford-ability: 25% at 50% SMSA median; 25% at 80% SMSA median; 50% at market	D	$ 8,123,369	$11,428,892	($3,305,523)	$ 8,123,369	$10,042,790	($1,919,421)
	E	$ 7,511,170	$11,060,557	($3,549,387)	$ 7,511,170	$ 9,751,366	($2,240,197)

* TDC includes all sales expenses and profit (if applicable to the scenario)

SALES ANALYSIS
NEW CONSTRUCTION - 152 UNITS

Affordability		I For-Profit Developer Sales Proceeds -	TDC =	Surplus (Gap)	II Non-Profit Developer Sales Proceeds -	TDC =	Surplus (Gap)
1/3 at 50% SMSA median; 1/3 at 80% SMSA median; 1/3 at market	A	$11,039,908	$22,301,732	($10,576,542)	$11,039,908	$19,537,299	($8,497,391)
	B	$13,117,606	$21,969,659	($8,852,053)	$13,117,606	$19,578,853	($6,461,247)
	C	$13,117,606	$21,168,111	($8,050,505)	$13,117,606	$18,772,427	($5,654,821)
35% affordability: 17½% at 50% SMSA median; 17½% at 80% SMSA median; 65% at market	D	$15,467,867	$22,008,926	($6,541,059)	$15,467,867	$19,318,041	($3,850,174)
50% affordability: 25% at 50% SMSA median; 25% at 80% SMSA median; 50% at market	E	$14,390,862	$21,650,429	($7,259,567)	$14,390,862	$19,456,204	($4,701,989)

* TDC includes all sales expenses and profit (if applicable to the scenario)

RENTAL ANALYSIS SUMMARY
NEW CONSTRUCTION - 100 UNITS

Affordability		I — For-Profit Developer		II — Non-Profit Developer	
		Gap - Yr. 1 First Year Breakeven	PV Gap after Subsidies ($Nominal)	GAP - Yr. 1 First Year Breakeven	PV Gap after Subsidies ($ Nominal)
1/3 at 50% SMSA median; 1/3 at 80% SMSA median; 1/3 at market	A	($ 967,206)	$ 7,813,152 (13,035,610)	($ 804,367)	$ 6,359,200 (10,568,179)
	B	($ 352,918)	$ 2,339,147 (3,686,946)	($ 342,929)	$ 2,246,331 (3,526,667)
	C	($ 306,301)	$ 1,925,496 (2,986,729)	($ 295,510)	$ 1,825,556 (2,814,382)
35% affordability: 17½% at 50% SMSA median; 17½% at 80% SMSA median; 65% at market	D	($ 407,398)	$ 2,141,989 (3,043,002)	($ 396,669)	$ 2,054,765 (2,903,520)
50% affordability: 25% at 50% SMSA median; 25% at 80% SMSA median; 50% at market	E	($ 340,341)	$ 1,885,332 (2,768,880)	($ 330,168)	$ 1,792,037 (2,608,655)

** Present Values (PV) are calculated over 15 years at 6.9% discount rate.

For-Profit Developer

Affordability		Land Contribution	SHARP	§.8/Ch. 707	Syndication	Total Subsidie
1/3 at 50% SMSA median; 1/3 at 80% SMSA median; 1/3 at market	A	0	0	0	$1,142,955	$1,142,9
	B	0	$1,503,694	$1,479,720	507,980	3,491,3
35% affordability: 17% at 50% SMSA median; 17½% at 80% SMSA median; 65% at market	C	$500,000	1,503,694	1,479,720	506,658	3,490,0
	D	270,000	808,722	786,738	0	1,595,4
50% affordability: 25% at 50% SMSA median; 25% at 80% SMSA median; 50% at market	E	375,000	1,120,369	1,086,350	372,176	2,578,8

Subsidy amounts for SHARP, §8/Ch. 707, and Syndication proceeds represent the present value of a 15 year stream, discounted at 6.9%.

SUBSIDY REQUIREMENT
RENTAL ANALYSIS
NEW CONSTRUCTION - 100 UNITS

II
Non-Profit Developer

Affordability		Land Contribution	SHARP	§.8/Ch. 707	Syndication	Total Subsidie
1/3 at 50% SMSA median; 1/3 at 80% SMSA median; 1/3 at market	A	0	0	0	$1,110,899	$1,110,8
	B	0	$1,503,694	$1,479,720	493,733	3,477,1
	C	$500,000	1,503,694	1,479,720	492,355	3,475,7
35% affordability: 17% at 50% SMSA median; 17½% at 80% SMSA median; 65% at market	D	270,000	808,722	786,738	0	1,595,4
50% affordability: 25% at 50% SMSA median; 25% at 80% SMSA median; 50% at market	E	375,000	1,120,369	1,086,350	361,746	2,568,4

Subsidy amounts for SHARP, $8/Ch. 707, and Syndication proceeds represent the present value of a 15 year stream, discounted at 6.9%.

ZONING

ZONING

The development program for the SENHI parcels was shaped in large part by a nine month community process Over fifteen meetings were held with South End residents and city representatives to gain community input on various program elements In addition, the BRA and the Mayor's Office of Neighborhood Services received over 50 letters from South End residents and organizations including specific comments and suggestions to improve the initiative

The major issues directly related to the financial feasibility study, and the general sense of those comments, are listed below

o Affordability - The preponderance of the comments received requested that a greater degree of affordability be established as the threshold requirement for the plan. Specifically, the majority of comments supported the requirement that one-third of the units produced be rented or sold to families with incomes at a below 50% of the SMSA median income, one-third at or below 80% of the SMSA median, and one-third at market levels.

A significant but lesser number of comments supported establishing a 35% limit on affordability Recommendations were also made for 100%, and 50% affordability.

o Gardens - Strong support was voiced for the community gardens A number of statements were made in support of maintaining all existing community gardens It was suggested that a committee of gardeners should plan the garden space at Parcel 6A as well as the current garden sites on other parcels.

o Technical Assistance - Comments suggested that the BRA should provide technical assistance to promote the development of Single Room Occupancy (SRO) residences and cooperatives Technical assistance should also be available to Community Development Corporations and non-profit organizations prior to the submission of proposals.

o Preference - Comments supported establishing a preference for minority business enterprises, community development corporations and non-profit groups or joint ventures between these groups and private developers Sentiment was also expressed in favor of South End developers with established track records A significant number of comments contended that South End property owners should be treated the same as MBEs, CDCs and non-profits

o Zoning and Land Use - Consensus was reached on the proposal that current zoning requirements should govern all developments Particular concern was raised about controlling density The Washington Street parcels should be dedicated to housing use, with some retail and commercial use allowed provided that it is limited

o Parking - Comments were split on the issue of parking. Generally,
   those supporting the "Community Compromise" suggested a parking
   requirement of .7 spaces per unit. A significant number of comments
   supported maintaining existing zoning requirements for parking

The community's comments indicate a clear view that all new development and
rehabilitation should conform to existing zoning and should provide the necessary parking, open space, and the quality of design and materials that are
typical of recent development projects in the South End   The community's
planning guidelines regarding zoning, design, parking, and open space do
have production cost implications   Since greater affordability can only be
achieved by lowering production costs, these planning guidelines limit the
field of cost factors that can be reduced to increase affordability   The
proposed number of residential units for the SENHI parcels conform to the
existing zoning code as delineated by the following density, open space,
height, and parking requirements. The only variances from the Code which
would be required by those scenarios would be for open space and yard
requirements

o Density - To determine the number of units allowed on each SENHI
   parcel under existing zoning, the allowable gross square footage of
   building was determined using the floor to area ratios (FAR) set by the
   Boston Zoning Code   Since the parcels all fall into H-2 or H-3 zones,
   the buildable square footage is either 2 or 3 times the land area, respec-
   tively   This number was divided then by the number of floors assumed
   possible for each site   Where specific recommendations were not available, an assumption of four floors was used   This yielded the square
   footage of the building footprint. This number and the product of the
   number of required parking spaces times 180 square feet were subtracted
   from the total parcel area in the case of vacant parcels to determine the
   amount of residual open space   As long as the amount of open space
   was at least 25 percent of that required by the Zoning Code, the number
   of units assumed was not reduced on the assumption that less open space
   in the South End is both acceptable and appropriate from an urban
   design perspective   In all cases the guidelines assume only residential
   units, and no commercial space.

o Height - The maximum height allowed for new construction in the South
   End is seventy (70) feet, and the minimum is thirty (30) feet. However, any new building must conform with the height and cornice line of
   adjacent buildings   Rehabilitation of existing buildings essentially must
   conform to the envelope of the existing building.

o Parking - The basic parking requirement assumed for each parcel is 7
   spaces per unit   For existing buildings, there is no parking requirement unless the proposed development varies from current use   For
   instance if more units than currently exist are proposed such as on
   Parcel SE-110 (the Allen House), then 5 parking spaces per unit would
   be required on every dwelling above the current number of units
   However, in all cases the 7 spaces per unit is sufficient to meet current
   zoning requirements

-15-

One exception to the methodology described above is the case of Parcels SE 59-66 where the methodology produced a density of 40 units, but staff architects advised that 30 units would be more realistic

Community Gardens

Two community garden sites, Parcel 30 (approximately 12,000 square feet) on Washington Street, known as the "gazebo site", and Parcel P-6A (approximately 47,000 square feet) known as the East Berkeley Street Gardens, will be maintained as garden sites   In preparing the SENHI development program, these community gardens are assumed to remain on their existing sites, and no housing is assumed for either of these parcels.

Historic Preservation and Urban Design

The South End of Boston is the largest essentially intact Victorian rowhouse neighborhood in America   Its predominant residential building type is the four or five story red brick rowhouse with elevated basement and mansard roof   The most prevalent style is the bow front. Angled bays and flat fronts are also found along many streets. Characteristic architectural features include decorative entrance canopies and iron-work, elaborate cornices, and granite and brownstone trim

The extraordinary degree of architectural homogeneity and coherence within the South End results primarily from the relatively short time span during which the area was developed   The majority of the land within the South End was created by filling mudflats and marshes to either side of a narrow neck along Washington Street which connected the colonial Boston settlement on the Shawmut peninsula to the mainland   Major boulevards with long vistas were laid out parallel to Washington Street   Cross streets which often focus on small squares created a more intimate scale   The harmonious South End streetscape was ensured by city stipulation of building setback, height and materials in the deeds which conveyed individual lots along the newly laid out streets

The physical character of the South End provides its diverse residents with a unique urban living experience   The small squares and parks enhance the neighborhood feeling and the long avenues provide an environment for commercial activity nearby   The pattern of stoops and small yards further encourage neighborly communication

The primary urban design objective is to create housing that reinforces the physical character and social diversity of the South End   Proposals will be reviewed for compatibility with existing use patterns and architecture in areas such as density, land coverage, height, materials, detailing, proportion and other elements that contribute to the distinctive historic character of the South End

-16-

Many of the parcels offered for development are within either the South End
Landmarks District or the adjacent South End Landmarks District Protection
Area   Development proposals for new construction and rehabilitation of
existing buildings within these areas must comply with the Standards and
Criteria of the Boston Landmarks Commission for the District   For parcels
located outside the boundaries of the Landmarks District, compliance with the
Standards and Criteria is nevertheless strongly encouraged

SENHI PARCEL PROFILES

#	Parcel Desc.	GSF*	FAR	No Flrs	No Units	Parking Spaces	Parking S F	Required Open Space	Residual Open Space	Building Footprint
Vacant Buildings										
1	SE-110	8,800	2	3	9	6	-	-	-	-
2	SE-116	11,900	3	4	13	9	-	-	-	-
3.	RR-121	6,000	2	3	6	4	-	-	-	-
4	SE-13	5,625	2	3	6	4	-	-	-	-
5	SE-72	14,300	2	4	15	11	-	-	-	-
6	SE-59-66	38,108	3	3	30	22	-	-	-	-
Sub Total		84,733			79	56	-	-	-	-
Vacant Lots										
7	P-6a**	47,516								
8	30**	12,000								
9	R11-C	7,947	2	4	16	11	1,980	2,400	1,994	3,974
10	RE-7B	44,920	2	3	89	62	11,160	13,350	3,813	29,947
11	29-A	24,024	2	4	48	34	6,120	7,200	5,892	12,012
12	R-12A	23,905	2	4	48	34	6,120	7,200	1,848	15,937
13	R-12B	15,090	2	3	30	21	3,780	4,500	3,765	7,545
14	33B	9,636	2	4	19	13	2,340	2,850	2,478	4,818
15.	SE-98A	1,075	2	4	2	1	180	300	358	538
Sub Total		186,113			252	176	31,680	37,800	20,148	74,771
TOTAL		270,846			331	232	31,680	37,800	20,148	74,771

* GSF for vacant buildings = Gross Floor Area of existing structures, for vacant parcels = parcel size

** Will be maintained as Garden Sites.

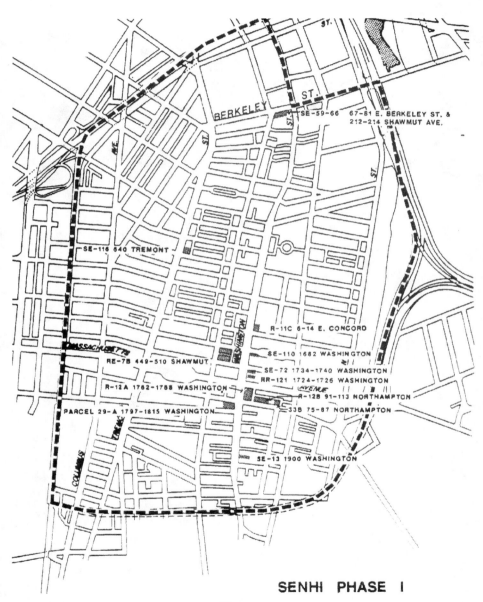

SE-59-66   67-81 E. BERKELEY ST. &
           212-214 SHAWMUT AVE.

SE-116 640 TREMONT

R-11C 6-14 E. CONCORD

SE-110 1682 WASHINGTON

RE-7B 449-510 SHAWMUT

SE-72 1734-1740 WASHINGTON

RR-121 1724-1726 WASHINGTON

R-12A 1782-1788 WASHINGTON

R-12B 91-113 NORTHAMPTON

PARCEL 29-A 1797-1815 WASHINGTON

33B 75-87 NORTHAMPTON

SE-13 1900 WASHINGTON

SENHI PHASE I

20

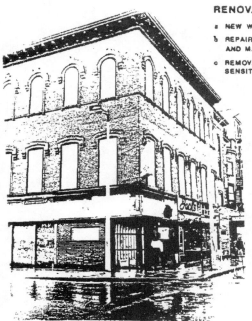

RENOVATION AND REHABILITATION

a NEW WINDOWS RECONSTRUCTING HISTORIC APPEARANCE

b REPAIR OF FACADE WITH SPECIAL EMPHASIS ON STONE
AND MASONRY DETAILING

c REMOVAL OF STOREFRONT AND SIGNAGE TREATMENT NOT
SENSITIVE TO ORIGINAL VICTORIAN DESIGN

1789 WASHINGTON

NEW DEVELOPMENT

1 USE OF MANSARD TO REDUCE BUILDING SCALE (HEIGHT)

2 BRICK MASONRY PREDOMINANT MATERIAL OF THE SOUTH END

3 USE OF DETAILS, PRECAST LINTELS AND SILLS, SPECIAL MASONRY
DETAILS, ORIALS AND BAYS TO DUPLICATE SOUTH END VERNACULAR

4 COMMERCIAL STOREFRONTS @ GRADE TO REINFORCE
GROUND FLOOR RETAIL WHERE APPROPRIATE

CAMDEN STREET   PARCEL 29A   NORTHAMPTON
STREET

NEW INFILL DEVELOPMENT

BUILDING HEIGHT
HEIGHT SHOULD BE CONSISTENT WITH
ESTABLISHED CORNICE LINES AND
MANSARDS.

STREET WALL
NEW DEVELOPMENT SHOULD FOLLOW
THE EXISTING SETBACKS AND
FRONTAGES.

FACADES
THE SCALE AND PROPRTION OF THE
EXISTING BUILDINGS IS TO BE
FOLLOWED. USE OF BAYS, MANSARDS,
STOOPS, AND ENTRY STAIRS IS
ENCOURAGED.

MATERIALS
MASONRY IS REQUIRED WITH THE USE
OF PRECAST CONCRETE, CAST IRON
AND WOOD TO ACCENT.

DETAILING
PRECAST LINTELS AND SILLS, BRICK
BANDING AND ACCENTS AND
CORNICES ARE REQUIRED TO ALLOW
NEW DEVELOPMENT TO BE COMPATIBLE
WITH EXISTING CHARACTER.

GAP ANALYSIS

GAP ANALYSIS

REHABILITATION- 79 SALES UNITS

SOUTH END NEIGHBORHOOD HOUSING INITIATIVE
PARCEL NUMBER: AGGREGATE OF ALL PHASE IA REHABS (#1-6)
PARCEL DESCRIPTION: SE-110, SE-116, R9-1.1, SE-1C, SE-78, SE-59-68.

PREPARED BY THE BOSTON REDEVELOPMENT AUTHORITY
===
DEVELOPMENT PROGRAM:

BUILDING AREA   85,374 GSF
PARCEL SIZE   18,196 SF
NUMBER OF UNITS   73 UNITS
PARKING SPACES   58 SPACES
EQUITY REQUIREMENT   15% OF TDC
===

UNIT MIX:

MARKET RATE   33 6% NO INCOME LIMIT
MODERATE INCOME   33 3% (NOT MORE THAN 80% OF SMSA MEDIAN INCOME)
LOW INCOME   33 3% (NOT MORE THAN 50% OF SMSA MEDIAN INCOME)
===

UNIT COMPOSITION:	NO UNITS	% AGE	GSF	NSF	EFFICIENCY
MARKET RATE					
1 BEDROOM UNITS	3	5.%	77	616	80.%
2 BEDROOM UNITS	15	5.%	1,195	850	80.%
TOTAL MARKET RATE UNITS	18	10.%	20,855	19,164	80.%
MODERATE INCOME					
2 BEDROOM UNITS	17	6.%	1,165	855	80.%
3 BEDROOM UNITS	8	10.%	1,345	1,476	80.0%
TOTAL MODERATE RATE UNITS	25	10.0%	30,210	24,156	80.0%
LOW INCOME					
2 BEDROOM UNITS	18	6.%	1,165	856	80.%
3 BEDROOM UNITS	12	10.%	1,345	576	80.%
TOTAL LOW INCOME UNITS	30	10.%	34,175	25,162	80.%
GRAND TOTAL	73		85,134	68,172	

===
DEVELOPMENT PRO FORMA

	UNIT COST	TOTAL COST
LAND COST:		
MARKET RATE UNITS	$35,000.00 DO PER	$9,0, 00
MODERATE INCOME UNITS	$10,000. 0 DO PER	$250,00
LOW INCOME UNITS	$5, 000.00 /DO PER	$155,00
TOTAL LAND COST		$1,115,000
HARD COSTS		
RESIDENTIAL CONSTRUCTION	$75 PER GSF	$6,401,500
TOTAL HARD COST & AC)		$6,400,500
PROJECT-RELATED SOFT COSTS:		
A&E FEE	5.% OF HC	$394,1
LEGAL FEES	2.% OF HC	$192,15
ACCOUNTING FEES	0.4% OF HC	$25,51
DEVELOPER'S FEE	4.0% OF HC	$256,2
PRESALE FEES (LOW/MOD UNITS ONLY)	$500 PER UNIT	$26,5
RE TAXES DURING CONSTRUCTION		$51,906
INSURANCE, TITLE, PERMITS		$64,005
MARKETING (MKT RATE UNITS)	$600 PER UNIT	$15,677
PROCESSING FEES (LOW/MOD UNITS)	$0 PER UNIT	$0
CONDO CARRYING COSTS (MKT UNITS)	10.00% PER YEAR	$105,607
CONSTRUCTION INTEREST	10.0 % PER YEAR	$270,646
TOTAL SOFT COSTS (SC)		$1,483,885
TOTAL PROJECT COSTS		$9,199,385
CONTINGENCY % HARD COSTS)	10.%	$640,050
TOTAL DEVELOPMENT COST		$9,925,435
EQUITY REQUIREMENT		$1,475,015
TDC/GSF		$115.05
TDC/1 BEDROOM UNIT		$88,748
TDC/2 BEDROOM UNIT		$124,74
TDC/3 BEDROOM UNIT		$155,1

MKT	33.%	
MOD	33.%	
LOW	33.0%	
NON PROFIT IF 1	0	
EMR LAND IF 1	0	
HOP IF 1	0	
NO LAND COST IF		
PTNRSHP IF 1	0	
NO EQUITY 1		
MKT PRICE NSF	$165	
EFFICIENCY	8.%	

```
REHABILITATION ANALYSIS     PERCENT MARKET RATE:      35.0%
PARCELS NUMBER 1 THRU 6      PERCENT MOD INCOME.       35.0%
OWNERSHIP SCENARIO.          PERCENT LOW INCOME.       33.0%
==============================================================

MARKET RATE SALES         PRICE/NSF =     $165

    1 BEDROOM UNITS         EACH   $101,640    $1,321,320
    2 BEDROOM UNITS         EACH   $140,580    $1,827,540
                                             ------------
GROSS SALES PROCEEDS OF MARKET RATE UNITS     $3,148,860
    LESS SALES EXPENSE               5.0%       $157,443
    LESS PRO RATA DEVELOPMENT COSTS           $2,749,283
    LESS RETURN ON SALES            15.0%       $472,329
NET PROFIT (GAP) AFTER SALES ==================>  ($230,201)

-------------------------------------------------------------
MODERATE INCOME SALES (80% OF MEDIAN INCOME)
    MAX ANNUAL MTG PAYMENT (FAM OF 4):   $5,440  (20% OF INCOME)
    MAX ANNUAL MTG PAYMENT (FAM OF 5):   $5,872  (20% OF INCOME)
                MORTGAGE INTEREST RATE:   9.00%
    DOWN PAYMENT PERCENT OF SALES PRICE.  5.00%
MAXIMUM SALES PRICE MODERATE INCOME:
    2 BEDROOM UNITS         EACH   $59,306    $1,008,209
    3 BEDROOM UNITS         EACH   $64,016      $576,145
                                             ------------
GROSS MODERATE INCOME SALES PROCEEDS          $1,584,354
    LESS SALES EXPENSE               2.0%        $31,687
    LESS PRO RATA DEVELOPMENT COSTS           $3,481,702
    LESS RETURN ON SALES            15.0%       $237,653
NET PROFIT (GAP) AFTER SALES ==================>  ($2,166,689)

         SALES PRICE/NSF 2 BEDROOMS:   $69.61
         SALES PRICE/NSF 3 BEDROOMS:   $59.43

-------------------------------------------------------------
LOW INCOME SALES (50% OF MEDIAN INCOME):
    MAX ANNUAL MTG PAYMENT (FAM OF 4):   $3,400  (20% OF INCOME)
    MAX ANNUAL MTG PAYMENT (FAM OF 5):   $3,670  (20% OF INCOME)
                         INTEREST RATE:   9.00%
    DOWNPAYMENT PERCENT OF SALES PRICE:   5.00%
MAXIMUM SALES PRICE LOW INCOME.
    2 BEDROOM UNITS         EACH   $37,067      $667,197
    3 BEDROOM UNITS         EACH   $40,010      $360,090
                                             ------------
GROSS LOW INCOME SALES PROCEEDS               $1,027,288
    LESS SALES EXPENSE               2.0%        $20,546
    LESS PRO RATA DEVELOPMENT COSTS           $3,504,444
    LESS RETURN ON SALES            15.0%       $154,093
NET PROFIT (GAP) AFTER SALES ==================>  ($2,751,795)

         SALES PRICE/NSF 2 BEDROOMS    $43.51
         SALES PRICE/NSF 3 BEDROOMS.   $37.18

-------------------------------------------------------------
GAP ANALYSIS:

PROFIT (GAP) FROM MARKET RATE SALES              ($230,201)

      1 BEDROOM UNITS.      PER UNIT   ($7,430)    ($96,593)
      2 BEDROOM UNITS:      PER UNIT  ($10,277)   ($133,604)

PROFIT (GAP) FROM MODERATE INCOME SALES         ($2,166,689)

      2 BEDROOM UNITS,      PER UNIT  ($76,383)  ($1,298,507)
      3 BEDROOM UNITS:      PER UNIT  ($96,465)    ($868,182)

PROFIT (GAP) FROM LOW INCOME SALES              ($2,751,795)

      2 BEDROOM UNITS:      PER UNIT  ($93,706)  ($1,686,712)
      3 BEDROOM UNITS       PER UNIT ($118,343)  ($1,065,083)
                                                ------------
TOTAL PROFIT (GAP) AFTER SALES ---------------->  ($5,148,684)
```

SOUTH END NEIGHBORHOOD HOUSING INITIATIVE
PARCEL NUMBER: AGGREGATE OF ALL PHASE 1A REHABS (#1-6)
PARCEL DESCRIPTION: SE-110, SE-115, RR-121, SE-13, SE-72, SE-59-68.

PREPARED BY THE BOSTON REDEVELOPMENT AUTHORITY
===

DEVELOPMENT PROGRAM:

BUILDING AREA	85,340 GSF
PARCEL SIZE	38,396 SF
NUMBER OF UNITS	79 UNITS
PARKING SPACES	55 SPACES
EQUITY REQUIREMENT	15% OF TDC

===

UNIT MIX:

MARKET RATE	33.0%	(NO INCOME LIMIT)
MODERATE INCOME	33.0%	(NOT MORE THAN 80% OF SMSA MEDIAN INCOME)
LOW INCOME	33.0%	(NOT MORE THAN 50% OF SMSA MEDIAN INCOME)

===

UNIT COMPOSITION:	NO. UNITS	% AGE	GSF	NSF	EFFICIENCY
MARKET RATE					
1 BEDROOM UNITS	13	50%	770	616	80.0%
2 BEDROOM UNITS	13	50%	1,065	852	80.0%
TOTAL MARKET RATE UNITS	26	100%	23,855	19,084	80.0%
MODERATE INCOME					
2 BEDROOM UNITS	17	67%	1,065	852	80.0%
3 BEDROOM UNITS	9	33%	1,345	1,076	80.0%
TOTAL MODERATE RATE UNITS	26	100%	30,210	24,168	80.0%
LOW INCOME					
2 BEDROOM UNITS	18	67%	1,065	852	80.0%
3 BEDROOM UNITS	9	33%	1,345	1,076	80.0%
TOTAL LOW INCOME UNITS	27	100%	31,275	25,020	80.0%
GRAND TOTAL	79		85,340	68,272	

===

DEVELOPMENT PRO FORMA

	UNIT COST	TOTAL COST
LAND COST:		
MARKET RATE UNITS	$35,000.00 /DU (FRV)	$910,000
MODERATE INCOME UNITS	$10,000.00 /DU (FRV)	$260,000
LOW INCOME UNITS	$5,000.00 /DU (FRV)	$135,000

TOTAL LAND COST -----------------------------) $1,305,000

HARD COSTS:		
RESIDENTIAL CONSTRUCTION	$75 PER GSF	$6,400,500

TOTAL HARD COSTS (HC) -----------------------) $6,400,500

PROJECT-RELATED SOFT COSTS:		
A/E FEE	6.0% OF HC	$384,030
LEGAL FEES	3.0% OF HC	$192,015
ACCOUNTING FEES	0.4% OF HC	$25,602
DEVELOPER'S FEE	4.0% OF HC	$256,020
TREGOR FEES (LOW/MOD UNITS ONLY)	$500 PER UNIT	$26,500
RE TAXES DURING CONSTRUCTION		$51,858
INSURANCE, TITLE, PERMITS	1.00% OF HC	$64,005
MARKETING (MKT RATE UNITS)	$600 PER UNIT	$15,600
PROCESSING FEES (LOW/MOD UNITS)	$0 PER UNIT	$0
CONDO CARRYING COSTS (MKT UNITS)	10.00% PER YEAR	$103,607
CONTRUCTION INTEREST	10.00% PER YEAR	$370,648

TOTAL SOFT COSTS (SC) -----------------------) $1,489,885

TOTAL PROJECT COSTS $9,195,385

CONTINGENCY (% HARD COSTS)	10.0%	$640,050

TOTAL DEVELOPMENT COST ============================) $9,835,435

EQUITY REQUIREMENT $1,475,315

TDC/GSF $115.25

TDC/1 BEDROOM UNIT	$88,740
TDC/2 BEDROOM UNIT	$122,741
TDC/3 BEDROOM UNIT	$155,011

MKT	33.0%
MOD	33.0%
LOW	33.0%
NON PROFIT IF 1	0
BMR LAND IF 1	0
HOP IF 1	1
NO LAND COST IF 0	1
PTNRSHP IF 1	0
NO EQUITY IF 0	
MKT PRICE/NSF	$185
EFFICIENCY	80.0%

```
==============================================================================

MARKET RATE SALES          PRICE/NSF =      $165

    1 BEDROOM UNITS          EACH   $101,640      $1,321,320
    2 BEDROOM UNITS          EACH   $140,580      $1,827,540
                                                  ----------
GROSS SALES PROCEEDS OF MARKET RATE UNITS         $3,148,860
    LESS SALES EXPENSE                    5.0%       $157,443
    LESS PRO RATA DEVELOPMENT COSTS                $2,749,289
    LESS RETURN ON SALES                 15.0%       $472,329
NET PROFIT (GAP) AFTER SALES ==================)   ($230,201)

------------------------------------------------------------------------------
MODERATE INCOME SALES (80% OF MEDIAN INCOME)
    MAX ANNUAL MTG PAYMENT (FAM OF 4).    $5,440  (20% OF INCOME)
    MAX ANNUAL MTG PAYMENT (FAM OF 5):    $5,870  (20% OF INCOME)
    MORTGAGE INTEREST RATE.               5.50%
    DOWN PAYMENT PERCENT OF SALES PRICE:  5.00%
MAXIMUM SALES PRICE MODERATE INCOME:
    2 BEDROOM UNITS           EACH   $84,044       $1,428,749
    3 BEDROOM UNITS           EACH   $90,713         $816,465
                                                  ----------
GROSS MODERATE INCOME SALES PROCEEDS              $2,245,213
    LESS SALES EXPENSE                    2.0%        $44,904
    LESS PRO RATA DEVELOPMENT COSTS                $3,481,705
    LESS RETURN ON SALES                 15.0%       $336,782
NET PROFIT (GAP) AFTER SALES ==================)  ($1,618,178)

            SALES PRICE/NSF 2 BEDROOMS:   $98.64
            SALES PRICE/NSF 3 BEDROOMS:   $84.31

------------------------------------------------------------------------------
LOW INCOME SALES (50% OF MEDIAN INCOME).
    MAX ANNUAL MTG PAYMENT (FAM OF 4):    $3,400  (20% OF INCOME)
    MAX ANNUAL MTG PAYMENT (FAM OF 5):    $3,670  (20% OF INCOME)
    INTEREST RATE.                        5.50%
    DOWNPAYMENT PERCENT OF SALES PRICE:   5.00%
MAXIMUM SALES PRICE LOW INCOME.
    2 BEDROOM UNITS           EACH   $52,528         $945,498
    3 BEDROOM UNITS           EACH   $56,699         $510,290
                                                  ----------
GROSS LOW INCOME SALES PROCEEDS                   $1,455,785
    LESS SALES EXPENSE                    2.0%        $29,116
    LESS PRO RATA DEVELOPMENT COSTS                $3,604,444
    LESS RETURN ON SALES                 15.0%       $218,368
NET PROFIT (GAP) AFTER SALES ==================)  ($2,396,142)

            SALES PRICE/NSF 2 BEDROOMS:   $61.65
            SALES PRICE/NSF 3 BEDROOMS:   $52.89

------------------------------------------------------------------------------
GAP ANALYSIS:

PROFIT (GAP) FROM MARKET RATE SALES               ($230,201)

    1 BEDROOM UNITS.         PER UNIT   ($7,430)     ($96,596)
    2 BEDROOM UNITS:         PER UNIT  ($10,277)    ($133,604)

PROFIT (GAP) FROM MODERATE INCOME SALES          ($1,618,178)

    2 BEDROOM UNITS:         PER UNIT  ($57,048)    ($969,781)
    3 BEDROOM UNITS.         PER UNIT  ($72,044)    ($648,395)

PROFIT (GAP) FROM LOW INCOME SALES               ($2,396,142)

    2 BEDROOM UNITS:         PER UNIT  ($81,595)   ($1,468,714)
    3 BEDROOM UNITS.         PER UNIT ($103,048)     ($927,428)
                                                  ----------
TOTAL PROFIT (GAP) AFTER SALES ---------------)  ($4,244,519)
```

SOUTH END NEIGHBORHOOD HOUSING INITIATIVE
        PARCEL NUMBER: AGGREGATE OF ALL PHASE 1A REHABS (#1-6)
        PARCEL DESCRIPTION. SE-110, SE-116, AR-121, SE-13, SE-72, SE-59-66.

PREPARED BY THE BOSTON REDEVELOPMENT AUTHORITY
===

I(c)

MKT	33.0%
MOD	33.0%
LOW	33.0%
NON PROFIT IF 1	0
BMR LAND IF 1	1
HOP IF 1	1
NO LAND COST IF 0	1
PTNRSHP IF 1	0
NO EQUITY IF 0	1
MKT PRICE/NSF	$165
EFFICIENCY	80 0%

DEVELOPMENT PROGRAM:

BUILDING AREA	85,340 GSF
PARCEL SIZE	38,398 SF
NUMBER OF UNITS	79 UNITS
PARKING SPACES	55 SPACES
EQUITY REQUIREMENT	15% OF TDC

===

UNIT MIX:

MARKET RATE	33.0%	(NO INCOME LIMIT)
MODERATE INCOME	33.0%	(NOT MORE THAN 80% OF SMSA MEDIAN INCOME)
LOW INCOME	33.0%	(NOT MORE THAN 50% OF SMSA MEDIAN INCOME)

===

UNIT COMPOSITION.	NO. UNITS	% AGE	GSF	NSF	EFFICIENCY
MARKET RATE					
1 BEDROOM UNITS	13	50%	770	616	80.0%
2 BEDROOM UNITS	13	50%	1,065	852	80.0%
TOTAL MARKET RATE UNITS	26	100%	23,855	19,084	80.0%
MODERATE INCOME					
2 BEDROOM UNITS	17	67%	1,065	852	80.0%
3 BEDROOM UNITS	9	33%	1,345	1,076	80 0%
TOTAL MODERATE RATE UNITS	26	100%	30,210	24,168	80.0%
LOW INCOME					
2 BEDROOM UNITS	18	67%	1,065	852	80.0%
3 BEDROOM UNITS	9	33%	1,345	1,076	80.0%
TOTAL LOW INCOME UNITS	27	100%	31,275	25,020	80.0%
GRAND TOTAL	79		85,340	68,272	

===

DEVELOPMENT PRO FORMA

	UNIT COST	TOTAL COST
LAND COST.		
MARKET RATE UNITS	$35,000.00 /DU (FRV)	$910,000
MODERATE INCOME UNITS	$0.00 /DU (FRV)	$0
LOW INCOME UNITS	$0.00 /DU (FRV)	$0
TOTAL LAND COST --------------------------)		$910,000
HARD COSTS:		
RESIDENTIAL CONSTRUCTION	$75 PER GSF	$6,400,500
TOTAL HARD COSTS (HC) -------------------)		$6,400,500
PROJECT-RELATED SOFT COSTS.		
A/E FEE	6 0% OF HC	$384,030
LEGAL FEES	3.0% OF HC	$192,015
ACCOUNTING FEES	0.4% OF HC	$25,602
DEVELOPER'S FEE	4.0% OF HC	$256,020
TREGOR FEES (LOW/MOD UNITS ONLY)	$500 PER UNIT	$26,500
RE TAXES DURING CONSTRUCTION		$49,200
INSURANCE, TITLE, PERMITS	1.00% OF HC	$64,005
MARKETING (MKT RATE UNITS)	$600 PER UNIT	$15,600
PROCESSING FEES (LOW/MOD UNITS)	$0 PER UNIT	$0
CONDO CARRYING COSTS (MKT UNITS)	10.00% PER YEAR	$98,880
CONTRUCTION INTEREST	10 00% PER YEAR	$353,748
TOTAL SOFT COSTS (SC) --------------------)		$1,465,602
TOTAL PROJECT COSTS		$8,776,102
CONTINGENCY (% HARD COSTS)	10.0%	$640,050
TOTAL DEVELOPMENT COST ===================)		$9,416,152
EQUITY REQUIREMENT		$1,412,423
TDC/GSF		$110.34
TDC/1 BEDROOM UNIT		$84,959
TDC/2 BEDROOM UNIT		$117,509
TDC/3 BEDROOM UNIT		$148,403

```
REHABILITATION ANALYSIS        PERCENT MARKET RATE:       33.0%
PARCELS NUMBER 1 THRU 6        PERCENT MOD INCOME:        33.0%
OWNERSHIP SCENARIO:            PERCENT LOW INCOME:        33.0%
=====================================================================

MARKET RATE SALES          PRICE/NSF =      $165

     1 BEDROOM UNITS          EACH   $101,640    $1,321,320
     2 BEDROOM UNITS          EACH   $140,580    $1,827,540

GROSS SALES PROCEEDS OF MARKET RATE UNITS            $3,148,860
   LESS SALES EXPENSE                    5.0%          $157,443
   LESS PRO RATA DEVELOPMENT COSTS                   $2,632,087
   LESS RETURN ON SALES                 15.0%          $472,329
NET PROFIT (GAP) AFTER SALES ====================)    ($112,999)

---------------------------------------------------------------------
MODERATE INCOME SALES (80% OF MEDIAN INCOME)
   MAX ANNUAL MTG PAYMENT (FAM OF 4):    $5,440   (20% OF INCOME)
   MAX ANNUAL MTG PAYMENT (FAM OF 5):    $5,872   (20% OF INCOME)
            MORTGAGE INTERTEST RATE:     5.50%
   DOWN PAYMENT PERCENT OF SALES PRICE:  5.00%
MAXIMUM SALES PRICE MODERATE INCOME:
     2 BEDROOM UNITS          EACH    $84,044    $1,428,749
     3 BEDROOM UNITS          EACH    $90,718      $816,463

GROSS MODERATE INCOME SALES PROCEEDS                 $2,245,213
   LESS SALES EXPENSE                    2.0%           $44,904
   LESS PRO RATA DEVELOPMENT COSTS                   $3,333,278
   LESS RETURN ON SALES                 15.0%          $336,782
NET PROFIT (GAP) AFTER SALES ====================)  ($1,469,752)

          SALES PRICE/NSF 2 BEDROOMS:    $98.64
          SALES PRICE/NSF 3 BEDROOMS:    $84.31

---------------------------------------------------------------------
LOW INCOME SALES (50% OF MEDIAN INCOME):
   MAX ANNUAL MTG PAYMENT (FAM OF 4):    $3,400   (20% OF INCOME)
   MAX ANNUAL MTG PAYMENT (FAM OF 5).    $3,670   (20% OF INCOME)
              INTEREST RATE:             5.50%
   DOWNPAYMENT PERCENT OF SALES PRICE:   5.00%
MAXIMUM SALES PRICE LOW INCOME.
     2 BEDROOM UNITS          EACH    $52,528      $345,496
     3 BEDROOM UNITS          EACH    $56,699      $510,290

GROSS LOW INCOME SALES PROCEEDS                     $1,455,785
   LESS SALES EXPENSE                    2.0%           $29,116
   LESS PRO RATA DEVELOPMENT COSTS                   $3,450,787
   LESS RETURN ON SALES                 15.0%          $218,368
NET PROFIT (GAP) AFTER SALES ====================)  ($2,242,485)

          SALES PRICE/NSF 2 BEDROOMS.    $61.65
          SALES PRICE/NSF 3 BEDROOMS:    $52.69

---------------------------------------------------------------------
GAP ANALYSIS:

PROFIT (GAP) FROM MARKET RATE SALES                   ($112,999)

     1 BEDROOM UNITS:       PER UNIT   ($3,647)      ($47,416)
     2 BEDROOM UNITS:       PER UNIT   ($5,045)      ($65,583)

PROFIT (GAP) FROM MODERATE INCOME SALES             ($1,469,752)

     2 BEDROOM UNITS:       PER UNIT  ($51,813)     ($880,829)
     3 BEDROOM UNITS:       PER UNIT  ($65,436)     ($588,922)

PROFIT (GAP) FROM LOW INCOME SALES                  ($2,242,485)

     2 BEDROOM UNITS:       PER UNIT  ($76,363)   ($1,374,530)
     3 BEDROOM UNITS:       PER UNIT  ($96,439)     ($867,955)

                                                    -----------
TOTAL PROFIT (GAP) AFTER SALES ----------------)   ($3,825,236)
```

SOUTH END NEIGHBORHOOD HOUSING INITIATIVE
        PARCEL NUMBER: AGGREGATE OF ALL PHASE 1A REHABS ($1-6)
        PARCEL DESCRIPTION: SE-110, SE-116, RR-121, SE-13, SE-72, SE-59-66.

PREPARED BY THE BOSTON REDEVELOPMENT AUTHORITY

I (d)
MKT   65.0%
MOD   17.5%
LOW   17.5%
NON PROFIT IF 1   0
BMR LAND IF 1   1
HOP IF 1   1
NO LAND COST IF 0   1
PTNRSHP IF 1   0
NO EQUITY IF 0   1
MKT PRICE/NSF $165
EFFICIENCY   80.0%

DEVELOPMENT PROGRAM:

BUILDING AREA	79,265 GSF	
PARCEL SIZE	38,396 SF	
NUMBER OF UNITS	79 UNITS	
PARKING SPACES	55 SPACES	
EQUITY REQUIREMENT	15% OF TDC	

UNIT MIX:

MARKET RATE	65.0%	(NO INCOME LIMIT)
MODERATE INCOME	17.5%	(NOT MORE THAN 80% OF SMSA MEDIAN INCOME)
LOW INCOME	17.5%	(NOT MORE THAN 50% OF SMSA MEDIAN INCOME)

UNIT COMPOSITION.	NO. UNITS	% AGE	GSF	NSF	EFFICIENCY
MARKET RATE					
1 BEDROOM UNITS	26	50%	770	616	80.0%
2 BEDROOM UNITS	25	50%	1,065	852	80.0%
TOTAL MARKET RATE UNITS	51	100%	46,645	37,316	80.0%
MODERATE INCOME					
2 BEDROOM UNITS	9	67%	1,065	852	80.0%
3 BEDROOM UNITS	5	33%	1,345	1,076	80.0%
TOTAL MODERATE RATE UNITS	14	100%	16,310	13,048	80.0%
LOW INCOME					
2 BEDROOM UNITS	9	67%	1,065	852	80.0%
3 BEDROOM UNITS	5	33%	1,345	1,076	80.0%
TOTAL LOW INCOME UNITS	14	100%	16,310	13,048	80.0%
GRAND TOTAL	79		79,265	63,412	

DEVELOPMENT PRO FORMA

	UNIT COST	TOTAL COST
LAND COST:		
MARKET RATE UNITS	$35,000.00 /DU (FRV)	$1,785,000
MODERATE INCOME UNITS	$0.00 /DU (FRV)	$0
LOW INCOME UNITS	$0.00 /DU (FRV)	$0
TOTAL LAND COST -------------------------)		$1,785,000
HARD COSTS:		
RESIDENTIAL CONSTRUCTION	$75 PER GSF	$5,944,875
TOTAL HARD COSTS (HC) -----------------)		$5,944,875
PROJECT-RELATED SOFT COSTS:		
A/E FEE	6.0% OF HC	$356,693
LEGAL FEES	3.0% OF HC	$178,346
ACCOUNTING FEES	0.4% OF HC	$23,780
DEVELOPER'S FEE	4.0% OF HC	$237,795
TRESOR FEES (LOW/MOD UNITS ONLY)	$500 PER UNIT	$14,000
RE TAXES DURING CONSTRUCTION		$52,022
INSURANCE, TITLE, PERMITS	1.00% OF HC	$59,449
MARKETING (MKT RATE UNITS)	$600 PER UNIT	$30,600
PROCESSING FEES (LOW/MOD UNITS)	$0 PER UNIT	$0
CONDO CARRYING COSTS (MKT UNITS)	10.00% PER YEAR	$217,150
CONTRUCTION INTEREST	10.00% PER YEAR	$369,009
TOTAL SOFT COSTS (SC) ----------------)		$1,538,843
TOTAL PROJECT COSTS		$9,268,718
CONTINGENCY (% HARD COSTS)	10.0%	$594,488
TOTAL DEVELOPMENT COST ================)		$9,863,206
EQUITY REQUIREMENT		$1,479,481
TDC/GSF		$124.43
TDC/1 BEDROOM UNIT		$95,814
TDC/2 BEDROOM UNIT		$132,521
TDC/3 BEDROOM UNIT		$167,363

```
REHABILITATION ANALYSIS        PERCENT MARKET RATE.         65.0%
PARCELS NUMBER 1 THRU 6        PERCENT MOD INCOME:          17.5%        I(d)
OWNERSHIP SCENARIO:            PERCENT LOW INCOME:          17.5%
============================================================================

MARKET RATE SALES          PRICE/NSF =        $165

    1 BEDROOM UNITS              EACH     $101,640     $2,642,640
    2 BEDROOM UNITS              EACH     $140,580     $3,514,500

GROSS SALES PROCEEDS OF MARKET RATE UNITS              $6,157,140
    LESS SALES EXPENSE                       5.0%        $307,857
    LESS PRO RATA DEVELOPMENT COSTS                    $5,804,191
    LESS RETURN ON SALES                    15.0%        $923,571
NET PROFIT (GAP) AFTER SALES ==================)       ($878,479)

-----------------------------------------------------------------------------
MODERATE INCOME SALES (80% OF MEDIAN INCOME)
    MAX ANNUAL MTG PAYMENT (FAM OF 4):      $5,440   (20% OF INCOME)
    MAX ANNUAL MTG PAYMENT (FAM OF 5):      $5,872   (20% OF INCOME)
             MORTGAGE INTERTEST RATE:        5.50%
    DOWN PAYMENT PERCENT OF SALES PRICE:     5.00%
MAXIMUM SALES PRICE MODERATE INCOME·
    2 BEDROOM UNITS                 EACH    $84,044     $756,397
    3 BEDROOM UNITS                 EACH    $90,718     $453,591

GROSS MODERATE INCOME SALES PROCEEDS                   $1,209,387
    LESS SALES EXPENSE                       6.0%        $24,606
    LESS PRO RATA DEVELOPMENT COSTS                    $2,029,507
    LESS RETURN ON SALES                    15.0%        $181,438
NET PROFIT (GAP) AFTER SALES ==================)     ($1,025,218)

              SALES PRICE/NSF 2 BEDROOMS:    $98.64
              SALES PRICE/NSF 3 BEDROOMS:    $84.31

-----------------------------------------------------------------------------
LOW INCOME SALES (50% OF MEDIAN INCOME),
    MAX ANNUAL MTG PAYMENT (FAM OF 4):      $3,400   (20% OF INCOME)
    MAX ANNUAL MTG PAYMENT (FAM OF 5).      $3,670   (20% OF INCOME)
                    INTEREST RATE:           5.50%
    DOWNPAYMENT PERCENT OF SALES PRICE·      5.00%
MAXIMUM SALES PRICE LOW INCOME:
    2 BEDROOM UNITS                 EACH    $52,528     $472,748
    3 BEDROOM UNITS                 EACH    $56,699     $283,434

GROSS LOW INCOME SALES PROCEEDS                         $756,242
    LESS SALES EXPENSE                       6.0%        $15,125
    LESS PRO RATA DEVELOPMENT COSTS                    $2,029,507
    LESS RETURN ON SALES                    15.0%        $113,436
NET PROFIT (GAP) AFTER SALES ==================)     ($1,401,826)

              SALES PRICE/NSF 2 BEDROOMS:    $61.65
              SALES PRICE/NSF 3 BEDROOMS:    $52.69

-----------------------------------------------------------------------------
GAP ANALYSIS·

PROFIT (GAP) FROM MARKET RATE SALES                    ($878,479)

    1 BEDROOM UNITS          PER UNIT  ($14,502)       ($377,043)
    2 BEDROOM UNITS·         PER UNIT  ($20,057)       ($501,437)

PROFIT (GAP) FROM MODERATE INCOME SALES              ($1,025,218)

    2 BEDROOM UNITS:         PER UNIT  ($66,944)       ($602,496)
    3 BEDROOM UNITS:         PER UNIT  ($84,544)       ($422,722)

PROFIT (GAP) FROM LOW INCOME SALES                   ($1,401,826)

    2 BEDROOM UNITS.         PER UNIT  ($91,536)       ($823,820)
    3 BEDROOM UNITS.         PER UNIT  ($115,601)      ($578,006)

                                                     -----------
TOTAL PROFIT (GAP) AFTER SALES ----------------)    ($3,305,523)
```

SOUTH END NEIGHBORHOOD HOUSING INITIATIVE
          PARCEL NUMBER: AGGREGATE OF ALL PHASE 1A REHABS (#1-6)
          PARCEL DESCRIPTION: SE-110, SE-116, RR-121, SE-13, SE-72, SE-59-66.

PREPARED BY THE BOSTON REDEVELOPMENT AUTHORITY
===
DEVELOPMENT PROGRAM.

     BUILDING AREA   82,155 GSF
     PARCEL SIZE   38,396 SF
     NUMBER OF UNITS   79 UNITS
     PARKING SPACES   55 SPACES
     EQUITY REQUIREMENT   15% OF TDC
===
UNIT MIX:

     MARKET RATE   50.0%   (NO INCOME LIMIT)
     MODERATE INCOME   25.0%   (NOT MORE THAN 80% OF SMSA MEDIAN INCOME)
     LOW INCOME   25.0%   (NOT MORE THAN 50% OF SMSA MEDIAN INCOME)
===

UNIT COMPOSITION:	NO UNITS	% AGE	GSF	NSF	EFFICIENCY
MARKET RATE					
1 BEDROOM UNITS	20	50%	770	616	80.0%
2 BEDROOM UNITS	19	50%	1,065	852	80.0%
TOTAL MARKET RATE UNITS	39	100%	35,635	28,508	80.0%
MODERATE INCOME					
2 BEDROOM UNITS	13	67%	1,065	852	80.0%
3 BEDROOM UNITS	7	33%	1,345	1,076	80.0%
TOTAL MODERATE RATE UNITS	20	100%	23,260	18,608	80 0%
LOW INCOME					
2 BEDROOM UNITS	13	67%	1,065	852	80.0%
3 BEDROOM UNITS	7	33%	1,345	1,076	80.0%
TOTAL LOW INCOME UNITS	20	100%	23,260	18,608	80.0%
GRAND TOTAL	79		82,155	65,724	

===
DEVELOPMENT PRO FORMA

	UNIT COST	TOTAL COST
LAND COST.		
MARKET RATE UNITS	$35,000.00 /DU (FRV)	$1,365,000
MODERATE INCOME UNITS	$0.00 /DU (FRV)	$0
LOW INCOME UNITS	$0.00 /DU (FRV)	$0
TOTAL LAND COST ----------------------------)		$1,365,000
HARD COSTS:		
RESIDENTIAL CONSTRUCTION	$75 PER GSF	$6,161,625
TOTAL HARD COSTS (HC) ----------------------)		$6,161,625
PROJECT-RELATED SOFT COSTS:		
A/E FEE	6.0% OF HC	$369,698
LEGAL FEES	3.0% OF HC	$184,849
ACCOUNTING FEES	0.4% OF HC	$24,647
DEVELOPER'S FEE	4.0% OF HC	$246,465
TREGOR FEES (LOW/MOD UNITS ONLY)	$500 PER UNIT	$20,000
RE TAXES DURING CONSTRUCTION		$50,654
INSURANCE, TITLE, PERMITS	1.00% OF HC	$61,616
MARKETING (MKT RATE UNITS)	$600 PER UNIT	$23,400
PROCESS NG FEES (LOW/MOD UNITS)	$0 PER UNIT	$0
CONDO CARRYING COSTS (MKT UNITS)	10.00% PER YEAR	$156,840
CONTRUCTION INTEREST	10.00% PER YEAR	$361,588
TOTAL SOFT COSTS (SC) ----------------------)		$1,499,756
TOTAL PROJECT COSTS		$9,026,381
CONTINGENCY (% HARD COSTS)	10 0%	$616,163
TOTAL DEVELOPMENT COST ======================)		$9,642,544
EQUITY REQUIREMENT		$1,446,382
TDC/GSF		$117.37
TDC/1 BEDROOM UNIT		$90,375
TDC/2 BEDROOM UNIT		$124,999
TDC/3 BEDROOM UNIT		$157,863

I(e)
MKT   50.0%
MOD   25.0%
LOW   25.0%
NON PROFIT IF 1   0
BMR LAND IF 1   1
HOP IF 1   1
NO LAND COST IF 0   1
PTNRSHP IF 1   0
NO EQUITY IF 0   1
MKT PRICE/NSF $165
EFFICIENCY   80.0%

```
==================================================================

MARKET RATE SALES        PRICE/NSF =    $165

   1 BEDROOM UNITS           EACH    $101,640       $2,032,800
   2 BEDROOM UNITS           EACH    $140,580       $2,671,020
                                                    -----------
GROSS SALES PROCEEDS OF MARKET RATE UNITS           $4,703,820
   LESS SALES EXPENSE                    5.0%         $235,191
   LESS PRO RATA DEVELOPMENT COSTS                  $4,182,485
   LESS RETURN ON SALES                 15.0%         $705,573
NET PROFIT (GAP) AFTER SALES ====================)   ($419,429)

------------------------------------------------------------------
MODERATE INCOME SALES (80% OF MEDIAN INCOME)
   MAX ANNUAL MTG PAYMENT (FAM OF 4):   $5,440   (20% OF INCOME)
   MAX ANNUAL MTG PAYMENT (FAM OF 5):   $5,872   (20% OF INCOME)
               MORTGAGE INTERTEST RATE:  5.50%
   DOWN PAYMENT PERCENT OF SALES PRICE:  5.00%
MAXIMUM SALES PRICE MODERATE INCOME:
   2 BEDROOM UNITS           EACH     $84,044       $1,092,573
   3 BEDROOM UNITS           EACH     $90,718         $635,027
                                                    -----------
GROSS MODERATE INCOME SALES PROCEEDS                $1,727,600
   LESS SALES EXPENSE                    2.0%          $34,552
   LESS PRO RATA DEVELOPMENT COSTS                  $2,730,029
   LESS RETURN ON SALES                 15.0%         $259,140
NET PROFIT (GAP) AFTER SALES ====================)  ($1,296,121)

         SALES PRICE/NSF 2 BEDROOMS:    $98.64
         SALES PRICE/NSF 3 BEDROOMS:    $84.31

------------------------------------------------------------------
LOW INCOME SALES (50% OF MEDIAN INCOME)
   MAX ANNUAL MTG PAYMENT (FAM OF 4):   $3,400   (20% OF INCOME)
   MAX ANNUAL MTG PAYMENT (FAM OF 5):   $3,670   (20% OF INCOME)
                      INTEREST RATE:     5.50%
   DOWNPAYMENT PERCENT OF SALES PRICE:   5.00%
MAXIMUM SALES PRICE LOW INCOME:
   2 BEDROOM UNITS           EACH     $52,528         $682,858
   3 BEDROOM UNITS           EACH     $56,699         $396,892
                                                    -----------
GROSS LOW INCOME SALES PROCEEDS                     $1,079,750
   LESS SALES EXPENSE                    2.0%          $21,595
   LESS PRO RATA DEVELOPMENT COSTS                  $2,730,069
   LESS RETURN ON SALES                 15.0%         $161,962
NET PROFIT (GAP) AFTER SALES ====================)  ($1,833,837)

         SALES PRICE/NSF 2 BEDROOMS:    $61.65
         SALES PRICE/NSF 3 BEDROOMS:    $52.69

------------------------------------------------------------------
GAP ANALYSIS:

PROFIT (GAP) FROM MARKET RATE SALES                  ($419,429)

   1 BEDROOM UNITS:          PER UNIT   ($9,063)     ($181,260)
   2 BEDROOM UNITS           PER UNIT  ($12,555)     ($238,169)

PROFIT (GAP) FROM MODERATE INCOME SALES             ($1,296,121)

   2 BEDROOM UNITS:          PER UNIT  ($59,345)     ($771,488)
   3 BEDROOM UNITS:          PER UNIT  ($74,948)     ($524,634)

PROFIT (GAP) FROM LOW INCOME SALES                  ($1,833,837)

   2 BEDROOM UNITS:          PER UNIT  ($83,965)   ($1,091,551)
   3 BEDROOM UNITS:          PER UNIT ($106,041)     ($742,286)
                                                    -----------
TOTAL PROFIT (GAP) AFTER SALES ------------------)  ($3,549,387)
```

SOUTH END NEIGHBORHOOD HOUSING INITIATIVE
           PARCEL NUMBER: AGGREGATE OF ALL PHASE 1A REHABS (#1-6)
           PARCEL DESCRIPTION. SE-110, SE-116, RR-1&1, SE-13, SE-72, SE-59-66.

PREPARED BY THE BOSTON REDEVELOPMENT AUTHORITY
===
DEVELOPMENT PROGRAM:

    BUILDING AREA   85,340 GSF
    PARCEL SIZE   38,396 SF
    NUMBER OF UNITS   79 UNITS
    PARKING SPACES   55 SPACES
    EQUITY REQUIREMENT   5% OF TDC
===
UNIT MIX:

    MARKET RATE   33.0% (NO INCOME LIMIT)
    MODERATE INCOME   33.0% (NOT MORE THAN 80% OF SMSA MEDIAN INCOME)
    LOW INCOME   33.0% (NOT MORE THAN 50% OF SMSA MEDIAN INCOME)
===

UNIT COMPOSITION:	NO. UNITS	% AGE	GSF	NSF	EFFICIENCY
MARKET RATE					
1 BEDROOM UNITS	13	50%	770	616	80.0%
2 BEDROOM UNITS	13	50%	1,065	852	80.0%
TOTAL MARKET RATE UNITS	26	100%	23,855	19,084	80.0%
MODERATE INCOME					
2 BEDROOM UNITS	17	67%	1,065	852	80.0%
3 BEDROOM UNITS	9	33%	1,345	1,076	80.0%
TOTAL MODERATE RATE UNITS	26	100%	30,210	24,168	80.0%
LOW INCOME					
2 BEDROOM UNITS	18	67%	1,065	852	80.0%
3 BEDROOM UNITS	9	33%	1,345	1,076	80.0%
TOTAL LOW INCOME UNITS	27	100%	31,275	25,020	80.0%
GRAND TOTAL	79		85,340	68,272	

===
DEVELOPMENT PRO FORMA
                                   UNIT COST   TOTAL COST
                                   =========   ==========
LAND COST:
    MARKET RATE UNITS $35,000.00 /DU (FRV) $910,000
    MODERATE INCOME UNITS $10,000.00 /DU (FRV) $260,000
    LOW INCOME UNITS $5,000.00 /DU (FRV) $135,000

TOTAL LAND COST ------------------------------------) $1,305,000

HARD COSTS:
    RESIDENTIAL CONSTRUCTION $75 PER GSF $6,400,500

TOTAL HARD COSTS (HC) ------------------------------) $6,400,500

PROJECT-RELATED SOFT COSTS,
    A/E FEE   4.0% OF HC $256,020
    LEGAL FEES   1.5% OF HC $96,008
    ACCOUNTING FEES   0.2% OF HC $12,801
    DEVELOPER'S FEE   4.0% OF HC $256,020
    TREGOR FEES (LOW/MOD UNITS ONLY) $500 PER UNIT $26,500
    RE TAXES DURING CONSTRUCTION $51,858
    INSURANCE, TITLE, PERMITS 1.00% OF HC $64,005
    MARKETING (MKT RATE UNITS) $600 PER UNIT $15,600
    PROCESSING FEES (LOW/MOD UNITS) $0 PER UNIT $0

    CONDO CARRYING COSTS (MKT UNITS) 10.00% PER YEAR $112,852
    CONSTRUCTION INTEREST   10.00% PER YEAR $403,005

TOTAL SOFT COSTS (SC) ------------------------------) $1,294,468

TOTAL PROJECT COSTS $8,999,968

CONTINGENCY (% HARD COSTS)   10.0% $640,050

TOTAL DEVELOPMENT COST ============================) $9,640,018

EQUITY REQUIREMENT $482,001

TDC/GSF $112.96

TDC/1 BEDROOM UNIT $86,979
TDC/2 BEDROOM UNIT $120,303
TDC/3 BEDROOM UNIT $151,931

MKT	33.0%
MOD	33.0%
LOW	33.0%
NON PROFIT IF 1	1
BAR LAND IF 1	0
HOP IF 1	0
NO LAND COST IF 0	1
PTNRSHP IF 1	0
NO EQUITY IF 0	1
MKT PRICE/NSF	$165
EFFICIENCY	80.0%

```
REHABILITATION ANALYSIS        PERCENT MARKET RATE:        20.0%
PARCELS NUMBER 1 THRU 6        PERCENT MOD INCOME:         50.0%
OWNERSHIP SCENARIO.            PERCENT LOW INCOME:         30.0%
================================================================

MARKET RATE SALES        PRICE/NSF =     $165

   1 BEDROOM UNITS          EACH    $101,640    $1,321,320
   2 BEDROOM UNITS          EACH    $140,580    $1,827,540

GROSS SALES PROCEEDS OF MARKET RATE UNITS           $3,148,860
   LESS SALES EXPENSE                   5.0%          $157,443
   LESS PRO RATA DEVELOPMENT COSTS                  $2,694,664
   LESS RETURN ON SALES                 0.0%               $0
NET PROFIT (GAP) AFTER SALES ==================        $296,753
----------------------------------------------------------------

MODERATE INCOME SALES (80% OF MEDIAN INCOME)
   MAX ANNUAL MTG PAYMENT (FAM OF 4).     $5,440   (20% OF INCOME)
   MAX ANNUAL MTG PAYMENT (FAM OF 5).     $5,872   (20% OF INCOME)
              MORTGAGE INTEREST RATE.     9.00%
   DOWN PAYMENT PERCENT OF SALES PRICE:   5.00%
MAXIMUM SALES PRICE MODERATE INCOME.
   2 BEDROOM UNITS          EACH    $59,306     $1,008,209
   3 BEDROOM UNITS          EACH    $64,015       $576,145

GROSS MODERATE INCOME SALES PROCEEDS                $1,584,354
   LESS SALES EXPENSE                   2.0%          $31,687
   LESS PRO RATA DEVELOPMENT COSTS                  $3,408,526
   LESS RETURN ON SALES                 0.0%               $0
NET PROFIT (GAP) AFTER SALES ==================    ($1,855,859)

        SALES PRICE/NSF 2 BEDROOMS:     $63.61
        SALES PRICE/NSF 3 BEDROOMS:     $53.49
----------------------------------------------------------------

LOW INCOME SALES (50% OF MEDIAN INCOME):
   MAX ANNUAL MTG PAYMENT (FAM OF 4):     $3,400   (20% OF INCOME)
   MAX ANNUAL MTG PAYMENT (FAM OF 5).     $3,670   (20% OF INCOME)
              INTEREST RATE:             9.00%
   DOWNPAYMENT PERCENT OF SALES PRICE.    5.00%
MAXIMUM SALES PRICE LOW INCOME:
   2 BEDROOM UNITS          EACH    $37,057       $667,137
   3 BEDROOM UNITS          EACH    $40,010       $360,090

GROSS LOW INCOME SALES PROCEEDS                     $1,027,238
   LESS SALES EXPENSE                   2.0%          $20,545
   LESS PRO RATA DEVELOPMENT COSTS                  $3,533,829
   LESS RETURN ON SALES                 0.0%               $0
NET PROFIT (GAP) AFTER SALES ==================    ($2,526,486)

        SALES PRICE/NSF 2 BEDROOMS.     $40.51
        SALES PRICE/NSF 3 BEDROOMS:     $37.18
----------------------------------------------------------------

GAP ANALYSIS:

PROFIT (GAP) FROM MARKET RATE SALES                   $296,753

   1 BEDROOM UNITS:        PER UNIT    $9,579     $124,523
   2 BEDROOM UNITS.        PER UNIT   $13,248     $172,230

PROFIT (GAP) FROM MODERATE INCOME SALES            ($1,859,859)

   2 BEDROOM UNITS:        PER UNIT  ($65,566)  ($1,114,622)
   3 BEDROOM UNITS:        PER UNIT  ($82,804)    ($745,238)

PROFIT (GAP) FROM LOW INCOME SALES                 ($2,526,086)

   2 BEDROOM UNITS.        PER UNIT  ($86,020)  ($1,548,364)
   3 BEDROOM UNITS         PER UNIT ($108,636)    ($977,720)

TOTAL PROFIT (GAP) AFTER SALES ---------------     ($4,089,192)
```

SOUTH END NEIGHBORHOOD HOUSING INITIATIVE
        PARCEL NUMBER, AGGREGATE OF ALL PHASE 1A REHABS (#1-b)
        PARCEL DESCRIPTION: SE-110, SE-116, RR-121, SE-13, SE-72, SE-59-66.

PREPARED BY THE BOSTON REDEVELOPMENT AUTHORITY
===

MKT	33.0%
MOD	33.0%
LOW	33.0%
NON PROFIT IF 1	1
BMR LAND IF 1	0
HOP IF 1	1
NO LAND COST IF 0	1
PTNRSHP IF 1	0
NO EQUITY IF 0	1
MKT PRICE/NSF	$165
EFFICIENCY	80.0%

DEVELOPMENT PROGRAM:

BUILDING AREA	85,340 GSF
PARCEL SIZE	38,396 SF
NUMBER OF UNITS	73 UNITS
PARKING SPACES	55 SPACES
EQUITY REQUIREMENT	5% OF TDC

===
UNIT MIX:

MARKET RATE	33.0%	(NO INCOME LIMIT)
MODERATE INCOME	33.0%	(NOT MORE THAN 80% OF SMSA MEDIAN INCOME)
LOW INCOME	33.0%	(NOT MORE THAN 50% OF SMSA MEDIAN INCOME)

===

UNIT COMPOSITION	NO UNITS	% AGE	GSF	NSF	EFFICIENCY
MARKET RATE					
1 BEDROOM UNITS	13	50%	770	616	80.0%
2 BEDROOM UNITS	13	50%	1,065	852	80.0%
TOTAL MARKET RATE UNITS	26	100%	23,855	19,084	80.0%
MODERATE INCOME					
2 BEDROOM UNITS	17	67%	1,065	852	80.0%
3 BEDROOM UNITS	9	33%	1,345	1,076	80.0%
TOTAL MODERATE RATE UNITS	26	100%	30,210	24,168	80.0%
LOW INCOME					
2 BEDROOM UNITS	18	67%	1,065	852	80.0%
3 BEDROOM UNITS	9	33%	1,345	1,076	80.0%
TOTAL LOW INCOME UNITS	27	100%	31,275	25,020	80.0%
GRAND TOTAL	79		85,340	68,272	

===
DEVELOPMENT PRO FORMA

	UNIT COST	TOTAL COST
LAND COST:		
MARKET RATE UNITS	$35,000.00 /DU (FRV)	$910,000
MODERATE INCOME UNITS	$10,000.00 /DU (FRV)	$260,000
LOW INCOME UNITS	$5,000.00 /DU (FRV)	$135,000
TOTAL LAND COST ----------------------)		$1,305,000
HARD COSTS:		
RESIDENTIAL CONSTRUCTION	$75 PER GSF	$6,400,500
TOTAL HARD COSTS (HC) --------------------------)		$6,400,500
PROJECT-RELATED SOFT COSTS:		
A/E FEE	4.0% OF HC	$256,020
LEGAL FEES	1.5% OF HC	$96,008
ACCOUNTING FEES	0.2% OF HC	$12,801
DEVELOPER'S FEE	4.0% OF HC	$256,020
TREGOR FEES (LOW/MOD UNITS ONLY)	$500 PER UNIT	$26,500
RE TAXES DURING CONSTRUCTION		$51,858
INSURANCE, TITLE, PERMITS	1.00% OF HC	$64,005
MARKETING (MKT RATE UNITS)	$600 PER UNIT	$15,600
PROCESSING FEES (LOW/MOD UNITS)	$0 PER UNIT	$0
CONDO CARRYING COSTS (MKT UNITS)	10.00% PER YEAR	$112,552
CONTRUCTION INTEREST	10.00% PER YEAR	$403,005
TOTAL SOFT COSTS (SC) ----------------------)		$1,294,468
TOTAL PROJECT COSTS		$8,999,968
CONTINGENCY (% HARD COSTS)	10.0%	$640,050
TOTAL DEVELOPMENT COST ======================)		$9,640,018
EQUITY REQUIREMENT		$482,001
TDC/GSF		$112.96
TDC/1 BEDROOM UNIT		$86,979
TDC/2 BEDROOM UNIT		$120,303
TDC/3 BEDROOM UNIT		$151,931

```
REHABILITATION ANALYSIS        PERCENT MARKET RATE.        33.0%
PARCELS NUMBER 1 THRU 6        PERCENT MOD INCOME.         33.0%
OWNERSHIP SCENARIO:            PERCENT LOW INCOME:         33.0%
=====================================================================

MARKET RATE SALES              PRICE/NSF =      $165

   1 BEDROOM UNITS             EACH   $101,640    $1,321,320
   2 BEDROOM UNITS             EACH   $140,580    $1,827,540

GROSS SALES PROCEEDS OF MARKET RATE UNITS            $3,148,860
   LESS SALES EXPENSE                        5.0%      $157,443
   LESS PRO RATA DEVELOPMENT COSTS                   $2,694,664
   LESS RETURN ON SALES                      0.0%           $0
NET PROFIT (GAP) AFTER SALES =================)       $296,753

---------------------------------------------------------------------
MODERATE INCOME SALES (80% OF MEDIAN INCOME)
   MAX ANNUAL MTG PAYMENT (FAM OF 4):   $5,440  (20% OF INCOME)
   MAX ANNUAL MTG PAYMENT (FAM OF 5):   $5,872  (20% OF INCOME)
             MORTGAGE INTEREST RATE:    5.50%
   DOWN PAYMENT PERCENT OF SALES PRICE: 5.00%
MAXIMUM SALES PRICE MODERATE INCOME.
   2 BEDROOM UNITS             EACH    $84,044    $1,428,749
   3 BEDROOM UNITS             EACH    $90,718      $816,462

GROSS MODERATE INCOME SALES PROCEEDS                 $2,245,210
   LESS SALES EXPENSE                        2.0%       $44,904
   LESS PRO RATA DEVELOPMENT COSTS                   $3,412,525
   LESS RETURN ON SALES                      0.0%           $0
NET PROFIT (GAP) AFTER SALES =================)     ($1,212,217)

           SALES PRICE/NSF 2 BEDROOMS:    $98.64
           SALES PRICE/NSF 3 BEDROOMS:    $84.31

---------------------------------------------------------------------
LOW INCOME SALES (50% OF MEDIAN INCOME),
   MAX ANNUAL MTG PAYMENT (FAM OF 4):   $3,400  (20% OF INCOME)
   MAX ANNUAL MTG PAYMENT (FAM OF 5):   $3,670  (20% OF INCOME)
                    INTEREST RATE:      5.50%
   DOWNPAYMENT PERCENT OF SALES PRICE.  5.00%
MAXIMUM SALES PRICE LOW INCOME.
   2 BEDROOM UNITS             EACH    $50,528      $945,496
   3 BEDROOM UNITS             EACH    $56,699      $510,290

GROSS LOW INCOME SALES PROCEEDS                      $1,455,785
   LESS SALES EXPENSE                        2.0%       $29,116
   LESS PRO RATA DEVELOPMENT COSTS                   $3,532,828
   LESS RETURN ON SALES                      0.0%           $0
NET PROFIT (GAP) AFTER SALES =================)     ($2,106,158)

           SALES PRICE/NSF 2 BEDROOMS    $61.85
           SALES PRICE/NSF 3 BEDROOMS:   $52.69

---------------------------------------------------------------------
GAP ANALYSIS.

PROFIT (GAP) FROM MARKET RATE SALES                   $296,753

   1 BEDROOM UNITS:            PER UNIT   $9,579     $124,520
   2 BEDROOM UNITS.            PER UNIT  $13,248     $172,230

PROFIT (GAP) FROM MODERATE INCOME SALES             ($1,212,217)

   2 BEDROOM UNITS:            PER UNIT ($42,725)    ($726,488)
   3 BEDROOM UNITS.            PER UNIT ($53,970)    ($485,730)

PROFIT (GAP) FROM LOW INCOME SALES                  ($2,106,158)

   2 BEDROOM UNITS:            PER UNIT ($71,781)  ($1,290,969)
   3 BEDROOM UNITS:            PER UNIT ($90,577)    ($815,189)

                                                    -----------
TOTAL PROFIT (GAP) AFTER SALES ---------------)     ($3,021,623)
```

SOUTH END NEIGHBORHOOD HOUSING INITIATIVE
    PARCEL NUMBER. AGGREGATE OF ALL PHASE 1A REHABS (#1-6)
    PARCEL DESCRIPTION· SE-110, SE-116, RA-121, SE-1C, SE-72, SE-59-66.

PREPARED BY THE BOSTON REDEVELOPMENT AUTHORITY
==

DEVELOPMENT PROGRAM.

BUILDING AREA	85,340 GSF	
PARCEL SIZE	38,396 SF	
NUMBER OF UNITS	79 UNITS	
PARKING SPACES	55 SPACES	
EQUITY REQUIREMENT	5% OF TDC	

MKT		33.0%
MOD		33.0%
LOW		33.0%
NON PROFIT IF 1		1
BMR LAND IF 1		1
HOP IF 1		1
NO LAND COST IF 0		1
PTNRSHP IF 1		0
NO EQUITY IF 0		1
MKT PRICE/NSF		$165
EFFICIENCY		80.0%

==

UNIT MIX:

MARKET RATE	33.0%	(NO INCOME LIMIT)
MODERATE INCOME	33.0%	(NOT MORE THAN 80% OF SMSA MEDIAN INCOME)
LOW INCOME	33.0%	(NOT MORE THAN 50% OF SMSA MEDIAN INCOME)

==

UNIT COMPOSITION·	NO. UNITS	% AGE	GSF	NSF	EFFICIENCY
MARKET RATE					
1 BEDROOM UNITS	13	50%	770	616	80.0%
2 BEDROOM UNITS	13	50%	1,065	852	80.0%
TOTAL MARKET RATE UNITS	26	100%	23,855	19,084	80.0%
MODERATE INCOME					
2 BEDROOM UNITS	17	67%	1,065	852	80.0%
3 BEDROOM UNITS	9	33%	1,345	1,076	80.0%
TOTAL MODERATE RATE UNITS	26	100%	30,210	24,168	80.0%
LOW INCOME					
2 BEDROOM UNITS	18	67%	1,065	852	80.0%
3 BEDROOM UNITS	9	33%	1,345	1,076	80.0%
TOTAL LOW INCOME UNITS	27	100%	31,275	25,020	80.0%

GRAND TOTAL	79		85,340	68,272	

==

DEVELOPMENT PRO FORMA

	UNIT COST	TOTAL COST
LAND COST:	===========	===========
MARKET RATE UNITS	$35,000.00 /DU (FRV)	$910,000
MODERATE INCOME UNITS	$0.00 /DU (FRV)	$0
LOW INCOME UNITS	$0.00 /DU (FRV)	$0
TOTAL LAND COST ----------------------------)		$910,000
HARD COSTS·		
RESIDENTIAL CONSTRUCTION	$75 PER GSF	$6,400,500
TOTAL HARD COSTS (HC) --------------------)		$6,400,500
PROJECT-RELATED SOFT COSTS·		
A/E FEE	4.0% OF HC	$256,020
LEGAL FEES	1.5% OF HC	$96,008
ACCOUNTING FEES	0.2% OF HC	$12,801
DEVELOPER'S FEE	4.0% OF HC	$256,020
TREGOR FEES (LOW/MOD UNITS ONLY)	$500 PER UNIT	$26,500
RE TAXES DURING CONSTRUCTION		$49,200
INSURANCE, TITLE, PERMITS	1.00% OF HC	$64,005
MARKETING (MKT RATE UNITS)	$600 PER UNIT	$15,600
PROCESSING FEES (LOW/MOD UNITS)	$0 PER UNIT	$0
CONDO CARRYING COSTS (MKT UNITS)	10.00% PER YEAR	$107,372
CONTRUCTION INTEREST	10.00% PER YEAR	$384,116
TOTAL SOFT COSTS (SC) ----------------------)		$1,267,641
TOTAL PROJECT COSTS		$8,578,141
CONTINGENCY (% HARD COSTS)	10.0%	$640,050
TOTAL DEVELOPMENT COST ==========================)		$9,218,191
EQUITY REQUIREMENT		$460,910
TDC/GSF		$108.02
TDC/1 BEDROOM UNIT		$83,173
TDC/2 BEDROOM UNIT		$115,038
TDC/3 BEDROOM UNIT		$145,283

REHABILITATION ANALYSIS   PERCENT MARKET RATE.   33.0%
PARCELS NUMBER 1 THRU 6   PERCENT MOD INCOME·   33.0%
OWNERSHIP SCENARIO: PERCENT LOW INCOME.   33.0%

```
========================================================================

MARKET RATE SALES        PRICE/NSF =      $165

    1 BEDROOM UNITS           EACH    $101,640     $1,321,320
    2 BEDROOM UNITS           EACH    $140,580     $1,827,540

GROSS SALES PROCEEDS OF MARKET RATE UNITS              $3,148,860
    LESS SALES EXPENSE                    5.0%          $157,443
    LESS PRO RATA DEVELOPMENT COSTS                   $2,576,751
    LESS RETURN ON SALES                  0.0%               $0
NET PROFIT (GAP) AFTER SALES ==================)         $414,666

------------------------------------------------------------------------
MODERATE INCOME SALES (80% OF MEDIAN INCOME)
    MAX ANNUAL MTG PAYMENT (FAM OF 4):   $5,440   (20% OF INCOME)
    MAX ANNUAL MTG PAYMENT (FAM OF 5)·   $5,672   (20% OF INCOME)
              MORTGAGE INTERTEST RATE.    8.50%
    DOWN PAYMENT PERCENT OF SALES PRICE   5.00%
MAXIMUM SALES PRICE MODERATE INCOME:
    2 BEDROOM UNITS           EACH     $84,044     $1,429,749
    3 BEDROOM UNITS           EACH     $90,719       $816,463

GROSS MODERATE INCOME SALES PROCEEDS                  $2,245,213
    LESS SALES EXPENSE                    2.0%          $44,904
    LESS PRO RATA DEVELOPMENT COSTS                   $3,263,201
    LESS RETURN ON SALES                  0.0%               $0
NET PROFIT (GAP) AFTER SALES ==================)     ($1,062,892)

           SALES PRICE/NSF 2 BEDROOMS:    $98.64
           SALES PRICE/NSF 3 BEDROOMS.    $84.31

------------------------------------------------------------------------
LOW INCOME SALES (50% OF MEDIAN INCOME):
    MAX ANNUAL MTG PAYMENT (FAM OF 4):   $3,400   (20% OF INCOME)
    MAX ANNUAL MTG PAYMENT (FAM OF 5):   $3,670   (20% OF INCOME)
                      INTEREST RATE:      8.50%
    DOWNPAYMENT PERCENT OF SALES PRICE:   5.00%
MAXIMUM SALES PRICE LOW INCOME:
    2 BEDROOM UNITS           EACH     $52,525       $945,496
    3 BEDROOM UNITS           EACH     $56,699       $510,290

GROSS LOW INCOME SALES PROCEEDS                       $1,455,785
    LESS SALES EXPENSE                    2.0%          $29,116
    LESS PRO RATA DEVELOPMENT COSTS                   $3,378,239
    LESS RETURN ON SALES                  0.0%               $0
NET PROFIT (GAP) AFTER SALES ==================)     ($1,951,569)

           SALES PRICE/NSF 2 BEDROOMS.    $61.65
           SALES PRICE/NSF 3 BEDROOMS     $52.69

------------------------------------------------------------------------
GAP ANALYSIS·

PROFIT (GAP) FROM MARKET RATE SALES                     $414,666

    1 BEDROOM UNITS:         PER UNIT   $13,385       $174,001
    2 BEDROOM UNITS:         PER UNIT   $18,512       $240,664

PROFIT (GAP) FROM MODERATE INCOME SALES             ($1,062,892)

    2 BEDROOM UNITS:         PER UNIT  ($37,470)      ($636,997)
    3 BEDROOM UNITS:         PER UNIT  ($47,322)      ($425,896)

PROFIT (GAP) FROM LOW INCOME SALES                  ($1,951,569)

    2 BEDROOM UNITS.         PER UNIT  ($66,456)    ($1,196,214)
    3 BEDROOM UNITS.         PER UNIT  ($83,928)      ($755,356)
                                                    ------------
TOTAL PROFIT (GAP) AFTER SALES -----------------)   ($2,599,796)
```

SOUTH END NEIGHBORHOOD HOUSING INITIATIVE
PARCEL NUMBER: AGGREGATE OF ALL PHASE 1A REHABS (#1-6)
PARCEL DESCRIPTION: SE-110, SE-116, RR-121, SE-13, SE-72, SE-59-66.

PREPARED BY THE BOSTON REDEVELOPMENT AUTHORITY
==

MKT		65.0%
MOD		17.5%
LOW		17.5%
NON PROFIT IF 1		1
BMR LAND IF 1		1
HOP IF 1		1
NO LAND COST IF 0		1
PTNRSHP IF 1		0
NO EQUITY IF 0		1
MKT PRICE/NSF		$165
EFFICIENCY		80.0%

DEVELOPMENT PROGRAM:

BUILDING AREA	79,265 GSF
PARCEL SIZE	38,396 SF
NUMBER OF UNITS	79 UNITS
PARKING SPACES	55 SPACES
EQUITY REQUIREMENT	5% OF TDC

==
UNIT MIX:

MARKET RATE	65.0%	(NO INCOME LIMIT)
MODERATE INCOME	17.5%	(NOT MORE THAN 80% OF SMSA MEDIAN INCOME)
LOW INCOME	17.5%	(NOT MORE THAN 50% OF SMSA MEDIAN INCOME)

==

UNIT COMPOSITION:	NO. UNITS	% AGE	GSF	NSF	EFFICIENCY
MARKET RATE					
1 BEDROOM UNITS	26	50%	770	616	80.0%
2 BEDROOM UNITS	25	50%	1,065	852	80.0%
TOTAL MARKET RATE UNITS	51	100%	46,645	37,316	80.0%
MODERATE INCOME					
2 BEDROOM UNITS	9	67%	1,065	852	80.0%
3 BEDROOM UNITS	5	33%	1,345	1,076	80.0%
TOTAL MODERATE RATE UNITS	14	100%	16,310	13,048	80.0%
LOW INCOME					
2 BEDROOM UNITS	9	67%	1,065	852	80.0%
3 BEDROOM UNITS	5	33%	1,345	1,076	80.0%
TOTAL LOW INCOME UNITS	14	100%	16,310	13,048	80.0%
GRAND TOTAL	79		79,265	63,412	

==
DEVELOPMENT PRO FORMA

	UNIT COST	TOTAL COST
LAND COST:		
MARKET RATE UNITS	$35,000.00 /DU (FRV)	$1,785,000
MODERATE INCOME UNITS	$0.00 /DU (FRV)	$0
LOW INCOME UNITS	$0.00 /DU (FRV)	$0
TOTAL LAND COST ----------------------)		$1,785,000
HARD COSTS.		
RESIDENTIAL CONSTRUCTION	$75 PER GSF	$5,944,875
TOTAL HARD COSTS (HC) ----------------------)		$5,944,875
PROJECT-RELATED SOFT COSTS:		
A/E FEE	4.0% OF HC	$237,795
LEGAL FEES	1.5% OF HC	$89,173
ACCOUNTING FEES	0.2% OF HC	$11,890
DEVELOPER'S FEE	4.0% OF HC	$237,795
TREGOR FEES (LOW/MOD UNITS ONLY)	$500 PER UNIT	$14,000
RE TAXES DURING CONSTRUCTION		$52,022
INSURANCE, TITLE, PERMITS	1.00% OF HC	$59,449
MARKETING (MKT RATE UNITS)	$600 PER UNIT	$30,600
PROCESSING FEES (LOW/MOD UNITS)	$0 PER UNIT	$0
CONDO CARRYING COSTS (MKT UNITS)	10.00% PER YEAR	$236,549
CONTRUCTION INTEREST	10.00% PER YEAR	$401,973
TOTAL SOFT COSTS (SC) ----------------------)		$1,371,246
TOTAL PROJECT COSTS		$9,101,121
CONTINGENCY (% HARD COSTS)	10.0%	$594,488
TOTAL DEVELOPMENT COST ======================)		$9,695,609
EQUITY REQUIREMENT		$484,780
TDC/GSF		$122.32
TDC/1 BEDROOM UNIT		$94,186
TDC/2 BEDROOM UNIT		$130,270
TDC/3 BEDROOM UNIT		$164,519

```
REHABILITATION ANALYSIS      PERCENT MARKET RATE:        65.0%
PARCELS NUMBER 1 THRU 6      PERCENT MOD INCOME.         17.5%
OWNERSHIP SCENARIO:          PERCENT LOW INCOME:         17.5%
===============================================================

MARKET RATE SALES          PRICE/NSF =      $165

     1 BEDROOM UNITS           EACH   $101,640      $2,642,640
     2 BEDROOM UNITS           EACH   $140,580      $3,514,500
                                                    ----------
GROSS SALES PROCEEDS OF MARKET RATE UNITS           $6,157,140
     LESS SALES EXPENSE                     5.0%      $307,857
     LESS PRO RATA DEVELOPMENT COSTS                $5,705,566
     LESS RETURN ON SALES                   0.0%           $0
NET PROFIT (GAP) AFTER SALES =====================)   $143,717
```

```
MODERATE INCOME SALES (80% OF MEDIAN INCOME)
     MAX ANNUAL MTG PAYMENT (FAM OF 4):    $5,440  (20% OF INCOME)
     MAX ANNUAL MTG PAYMENT (FAM OF 3):    $5,672  (20% OF INCOME)
          MORTGAGE INTEREST RATE:          5.50%
     DOWN PAYMENT PERCENT OF SALES PRICE:  5.00%
MAXIMUM SALES PRICE MODERATE INCOME:
     2 BEDROOM UNITS           EACH    $84,044       $756,397
     3 BEDROOM UNITS           EACH    $90,718       $453,591
                                                    ----------
GROSS MODERATE INCOME SALES PROCEEDS               $1,209,987
     LESS SALES EXPENSE                     2.0%      $24,200
     LESS PRO RATA DEVELOPMENT COSTS               $1,995,021
     LESS RETURN ON SALES                   0.0%           $0
NET PROFIT (GAP) AFTER SALES =====================  ($809,234)

          SALES PRICE/NSF 2 BEDROOMS.     $98.64
          SALES PRICE/NSF 3 BEDROOMS.     $84.31
```

```
LOW INCOME SALES (50% OF MEDIAN INCOME):
     MAX ANNUAL MTG PAYMENT (FAM OF 4):    $3,400  (20% OF INCOME)
     MAX ANNUAL MTG PAYMENT (FAM OF 5):    $3,670  (20% OF INCOME)
          INTEREST RATE                    5.50%
     DOWNPAYMENT PERCENT OF SALES PRICE:   5.00%
MAXIMUM SALES PRICE LOW INCOME:
     2 BEDROOM UNITS           EACH    $52,528       $472,748
     3 BEDROOM UNITS           EACH    $56,599       $283,494
                                                    ----------
GROSS LOW INCOME SALES PROCEEDS                      $756,242
     LESS SALES EXPENSE                     2.0%      $15,125
     LESS PRO RATA DEVELOPMENT COSTS               $1,995,021
     LESS RETURN ON SALES                   0.0%           $0
NET PROFIT (GAP) AFTER SALES =====================) ($1,253,904)

          SALES PRICE/NSF 2 BEDROOMS:     $61.65
          SALES PRICE/NSF 3 BEDROOMS     $52.69
```

```
GAP ANALYSIS:

PROFIT (GAP) FROM MARKET RATE SALES                  $143,717

     1 BEDROOM UNITS:        PER UNIT    $2,372       $61,680
     2 BEDROOM UNITS:        PER UNIT    $3,281       $82,034

PROFIT (GAP) FROM MODERATE INCOME SALES             ($809,234)

     2 BEDROOM UNITS:        PER UNIT   ($52,841)    ($475,567)
     3 BEDROOM UNITS:        PER UNIT   ($66,703)    ($333,666)

PROFIT (GAP) FROM LOW INCOME SALES                ($1,253,904)

     2 BEDROOM UNITS.        PER UNIT   ($61,877)    ($736,890)
     3 BEDROOM UNITS:        PER UNIT  ($103,403)    ($517,014)
                                                    ----------
TOTAL PROFIT (GAP) AFTER SALES -----------------,  ($1,919,421)
```

SOUTH END NEIGHBORHOOD HOUSING INITIATIVE
          PARCEL NUMBER: AGGREGATE OF ALL PHASE 1A REHABS (#1-6)
          PARCEL DESCRIPTION: SE-110, SE-116, RR-121, SE-13, SE-7C, SE-59-66.

PREPARED BY THE BOSTON REDEVELOPMENT AUTHORITY
===
DEVELOPMENT PROGRAM:

    BUILDING AREA   82,155 GSF
    PARCEL SIZE   38,396 SF
    NUMBER OF UNITS   79 UNITS
    PARKING SPACES   55 SPACES
    EQUITY REQUIREMENT   5% OF TDC
===
UNIT MIX:

    MARKET RATE   50.0% (NO INCOME LIMIT)
    MODERATE INCOME   25.0% (NOT MORE THAN 80% OF SMSA MEDIAN INCOME)
    LOW INCOME   25.0% (NOT MORE THAN 50% OF SMSA MEDIAN INCOME)
===

UNIT COMPOSITION:	NO. UNITS	% AGE	GSF	NSF	EFFICIENCY
MARKET RATE					
1 BEDROOM UNITS	20	50%	770	616	80.0%
2 BEDROOM UNITS	19	50%	1,065	852	80.0%
TOTAL MARKET RATE UNITS	39	100%	35,635	28,508	80.0%
MODERATE INCOME					
2 BEDROOM UNITS	13	67%	1,065	852	80.0%
3 BEDROOM UNITS	7	33%	1,345	1,076	80.0%
TOTAL MODERATE RATE UNITS	20	100%	23,260	18,608	80.0%
LOW INCOME					
2 BEDROOM UNITS	13	67%	1,065	852	80.0%
3 BEDROOM UNITS	7	33%	1,345	1,076	80.0%
TOTAL LOW INCOME UNITS	20	100%	23,260	18,608	80.0%
GRAND TOTAL	79		82,155	65,724	

===
DEVELOPMENT PRO FORMA

	UNIT COST	TOTAL COST
LAND COST.		
MARKET RATE UNITS	$35,000.00 /DU (FRV)	$1,365,000
MODERATE INCOME UNITS	$0.00 /DU (FRV)	$0
LOW INCOME UNITS	$0.00 /DU (FRV)	$0

TOTAL LAND COST --------------------------------------) $1,365,000

HARD COSTS:		
RESIDENTIAL CONSTRUCTION	$75 PER GSF	$6,161,625

TOTAL HARD COSTS (HC) ------------------------------) $6,161,625

PROJECT-RELATED SOFT COSTS:		
A/E FEE	4.0% OF HC	$246,465
LEGAL FEES	1.5% OF HC	$92,424
ACCOUNTING FEES	0.2% OF HC	$12,323
DEVELOPER'S FEE	4.0% OF HC	$246,465
TREBOR FEES (LOW/MOD UNITS ONLY)	$500 PER UNIT	$20,000
RE TAXES DURING CONSTRUCTION		$50,654
INSURANCE, TITLE, PERMITS	1.00% OF HC	$61,616
MARKETING (MKT RATE UNITS)	$600 PER UNIT	$23,400
PROCESSING FEES (LOW/MOD UNITS)	$0 PER UNIT	$0
CONDO CARRYING COSTS (MKT UNITS)	10.00% PER YEAR	$170,595
CONTRUCTION INTEREST	10.00% PER YEAR	$393,299

TOTAL SOFT COSTS (SC) ------------------------------) $1,317,241

TOTAL PROJECT COSTS $8,843,866

CONTINGENCY (% HARD COSTS)   10.0% $616,163

TOTAL DEVELOPMENT COST =============================) $9,460,029

EQUITY REQUIREMENT $473,001

TDC/GSF $115.15

TDC/1 BEDROOM UNIT	$88,664
TDC/2 BEDROOM UNIT	$122,633
TDC/3 BEDROOM UNIT	$154,875

MKT	50.0%
MOD	25.0%
LOW	25.0%
NON PROFIT IF 1	1
BMR LAND IF 1	1
HDP IF 1	1
NO LAND COST IF 0	1
PTNRSHP IF 1	0
NO EQUITY IF 0	1
MKT PRICE/NSF	$165
EFFICIENCY	80.0%

```
REHABILITATION ANALYSIS        PERCENT MARKET RATE.         50.0%
PARCELS NUMBER 1 THRU 6        PERCENT MOD INCOME:          25.0%
OWNERSHIP SCENARIO:            PERCENT LOW INCOME.          25.0%
================================================================

MARKET RATE SALES         PRICE/NSF =    $165

    1 BEDROOM UNITS            EACH     $101,640     $2,032,800
    2 BEDROOM UNITS            EACH     $140,580     $2,671,020
                                                     ----------
GROSS SALES PROCEEDS OF MARKET RATE UNITS            $4,703,820
    LESS SALES EXPENSE                      5.0%       $235,191
    LESS PRO RATA DEVELOPMENT COSTS                  $4,103,318
    LESS RETURN ON SALES                    0.0%             $0
NET PROFIT (GAP) AFTER SALES ================)         $365,311

----------------------------------------------------------------

MODERATE INCOME SALES (80% OF MEDIAN INCOME)
    MAX ANNUAL MTG PAYMENT (FAM OF 4).      $5,440  (20% OF INCOME)
    MAX ANNUAL MTG PAYMENT (FAM OF 5):      $5,872  (20% OF INCOME)
            MORTGAGE INTERTEST RATE.         5.50%
    DOWN PAYMENT PERCENT OF SALES PRICE:     5 00%
MAXIMUM SALES PRICE MODERATE INCOME:
    2 BEDROOM UNITS            EACH      $84,044     $1,092,573
    3 BEDROOM UNITS            EACH      $90,718       $635,027
                                                     ----------
GROSS MODERATE INCOME SALES PROCEEDS                 $1,727,600
    LESS SALES EXPENSE                      2.0%        $34,552
    LESS PRO RATA DEVELOPMENT COSTS                  $2,678,355
    LESS RETURN ON SALES                    0 0%             $0
NET PROFIT (GAP) AFTER SALES ================)       ($985,307)

            SALES PRICE/NSF 2 BEDROOMS:       $98.64
            SALES PRICE/NSF 3 BEDROOMS.       $84.31

----------------------------------------------------------------

LOW INCOME SALES (50% OF MEDIAN INCOME).
    MAX ANNUAL MTG PAYMENT (FAM OF 4):      $3,400  (20% OF INCOME)
    MAX ANNUAL MTG PAYMENT (FAM OF 5):      $3,670  (20% OF INCOME)
                    INTEREST RATE.           5.50%
    DOWNPAYMENT PERCENT OF SALES PRICE.      5.00%
MAXIMUM SALES PRICE LOW INCOME:
    2 BEDROOM UNITS            EACH      $52,528       $682,858
    3 BEDROOM UNITS            EACH      $56,699       $396,892
                                                     ----------
GROSS LOW INCOME SALES PROCEEDS                      $1,079,750
    LESS SALES EXPENSE                      2.0%        $21,595
    LESS PRO RATA DEVELOPMENT COSTS                  $2,678,355
    LESS RETURN ON SALES                    0.0%             $0
NET PROFIT (GAP) AFTER SALES ================)     ($1,620,200)

            SALES PRICE/NSF 2 BEDROOMS:       $61.65
            SALES PRICE/NSF 3 BEDROOMS·       $52 69

----------------------------------------------------------------

GAP ANALYSIS·

PROFIT (GAP) FROM MARKET RATE SALES                    $365,311

    1 BEDROOM UNITS.          PER UNIT     $7,894       $157,872
    2 BEDROOM UNITS:          PER UNIT    $10,318       $207,438

PROFIT (GAP) FROM MODERATE INCOME SALES              ($985,307)

    2 BEDROOM UNITS.          PER UNIT   ($45,114)    ($586,482)
    3 BEDROOM UNITS:          PER UNIT   ($56,975)    ($398,825)

PROFIT (GAP) FROM LOW INCOME SALES                 ($1,620,200)

    2 BEDROOM UNITS.          PER UNIT   ($74,184)    ($964,388)
    3 BEDROOM UNITS:          PER UNIT   ($93,687)    ($655,812)
                                                     ----------
TOTAL PROFIT (GAP) AFTER SALES --------------)     $2,240,197)
```

GAP ANALYSIS

NEW CONSTRUCTION - 152 SALES UNITS

        PARCEL NUMBER: AGGREGATE OF ALL PHASE 1B VACANT LOTS (#9 - 15)
        PARCEL DESCRIPTION: R11-C, RE-78, 29-A, R-12A, R-12B, 338, SE-98A.

PREPARED BY THE BOSTON REDEVELOPMENT AUTHORITY
==

			CASE Ia	
DEVELOPMENT PROGRAM:			MKT	33.0%
BUILDING SIZE	152,285		MOD	33.0%
PARCEL SIZE	76,360 SF		LOW	33.0%
NUMBER OF UNITS	152 UNITS		NON PROFIT IF 1	0
PARKING SPACES	106 SPACES		BMR LAND IF 1	0
EQUITY REQUIREMENT	15% OF TDC		HOP IF 1	0

CASE Ia
MKT   33.0%
MOD   33.0%
LOW   33.0%
NON PROFIT IF 1   0
BMR LAND IF 1   0
HOP IF 1   0
NO LAND COST IF 0   1
PTNRSHP IF 1   0
NO EQUITY IF 0   1
MKT PRICE/NSF $165
EFFICIENCY   85.0%

==
UNIT MIX:

MARKET RATE	33.0%	(NO INCOME LIMIT)
MODERATE INCOME	33.0%	(NOT MORE THAN 80% OF SMSA MEDIAN INCOME)
LOW INCOME	33.0%	(NOT MORE THAN 50% OF SMSA MEDIAN INCOME)

==

UNIT COMPOSITION.	NO. UNITS	% AGE	GSF	NSF	EFFICIENCY
MARKET RATE					
1 BEDROOM UNITS	26	50%	700	595	85.0%
2 BEDROOM UNITS	25	50%	1,000	850	85.0%
TOTAL MARKET RATE UNITS	51	100%	43,200	36,720	85.0%
MODERATE INCOME					
2 BEDROOM UNITS	34	67%	1,000	850	85.0%
3 BEDROOM UNITS	16	33%	1,245	1,058	85.0%
TOTAL MODERATE RATE UNITS	50	100%	53,920	45,832	85.0%
LOW INCOME					
2 BEDROOM UNITS	34	67%	1,000	850	85.0%
3 BEDROOM UNITS	17	33%	1,245	1,058	85.0%
TOTAL LOW INCOME UNITS	51	100%	55,165	46,890	85.0%
GRAND TOTAL	152		152,285	129,442	

==
DEVELOPMENT PRO FORMA

	UNIT COST	TOTAL COST
LAND COST:	============	============
MARKET RATE UNITS	$25,000 /DU (FMV)	$1,275,000
MODERATE INCOME UNITS	$10,000 /DU (FMV)	$500,000
LOW INCOME UNITS	$5,000 /DU (FMV)	$255,000
TOTAL LAND COST ----------------------------)		$2,030,000
HARD COSTS:		
RESIDENTIAL CONSTRUCTION	$90 PER GSF	$13,705,650
TOTAL HARD COSTS (HC) ---------------------)		$13,705,650
PROJECT-RELATED SOFT COSTS		
A/E FEE	6.0% OF HC	$822,339
LEGAL FEES	3.0% OF HC	$411,170
ACCOUNTING FEES	0.4% OF HC	$54,823
DEVELOPER'S FEE	4.0% OF HC	$548,226
LESSOR FEES (LOW/MOD UNITS ONLY)	$500 PER UNIT	$50,500
RE TAXES DURING CONSTRUCTION		$195,301
INSURANCE, TITLE, PERMITS	1.0% OF HC	$137,057
MARKETING (MKT RATE UNITS)	$600 PER UNIT	$30,600
PROCESSING FEES (LOW/MOD UNITS)	$0 PER UNIT	$0
CONDO CARRYING COSTS (MKT UNITS)	10.00% PER YEAR	$215,760
CONTRUCTION INTEREST	10.00% PER YEAR	$760,591
TOTAL SOFT COSTS (SC) -----------------------		$3,036,363
TOTAL PROJECT COSTS		$18,872,013
CONTINGENCY (% HARD COSTS)	5.0%	$685,283
TOTAL DEVELOPMENT COST ====================)		$19,557,302
EQUITY REQUIREMENT		$2,300,885
TDC/GSF		$128.43
TDC/1 BEDROOM UNIT		$89,901
TDC/2 BEDROOM UNIT		$128,430
TDC/3 BEDROOM UNIT		$159,835

-41-

```
NEW CONSTRUCTION ANALYSIS      PERCENT MARKET RATE.          33.0%
PARCELS NUMBER 9 THRU 15       PERCENT MOD INCOME:           33.0%
OWNERSHIP SCENARIO·            PERCENT LOW INCOME:           33.0%
============================================================

MARKET RATE SALES          PRICE/NSF =        $165

    1 BEDROOM UNITS            EACH    $98,175       $2,552,550
    2 BEDROOM UNITS            EACH   $140,250       $3,506,250

GROSS SALES PROCEEDS OF MARKET RATE UNITS            $6,058,800
    LESS SALES EXPENSE                    5.0%         $302,940
    LESS PRO RATA DEVELOPMENT COSTS                  $5,548,159
    LESS RETURN ON SALES                 15.0%         $908,820
NET PROFIT (GAP) AFTER SALES =================)       ($701,119)
------------------------------------------------------------

MODERATE INCOME SALES (80% OF MEDIAN INCOME)
    MAX ANNUAL MTG PAYMENT (FAM OF 4)·     $5,440  (20% OF INCOME)
    MAX ANNUAL MTG PAYMENT (FAM OF 5):     $5,672  (20% OF INCOME)
            MORTGAGE INTERTEST RATE·       9.00%
    DOWN PAYMENT PERCENT OF SALES PRICE:   5.00%
MAXIMUM SALES PRICE MODERATE INCOME:
    2 BEDROOM UNITS            EACH    $59,306       $2,016,419
    3 BEDROOM UNITS            EACH    $64,016       $1,024,057

GROSS MODERATE INCOME SALES PROCEEDS                 $3,040,876
    LESS SALES EXPENSE                    2.0%          $60,814
    LESS PRO RATA DEVELOPMENT COSTS                  $6,924,324
    LESS RETURN ON SALES                 15.0%         $456,101
NET PROFIT (GAP) AFTER SALES ==================)    ($4,401,163)

            SALES PRICE/NSF 2 BEDROOMS:    $69.77
            SALES PRICE/NSF 3 BEDROOMS:    $60.49
------------------------------------------------------------

LOW INCOME SALES (50% OF MEDIAN INCOME):
    MAX ANNUAL MTG PAYMENT (FAM OF 4).     $3,400  (20% OF INCOME)
    MAX ANNUAL MTG PAYMENT (FAM OF 5):     $3,670  (21% OF INCOME)
            INTEREST RATE:                 3.00%
    DOWNPAYMENT PERCENT OF SALES PRICE·    5.00%
MAXIMUM SALES PRICE LOW INCOME·
    2 BEDROOM UNITS            EACH    $37,767       $1,260,262
    3 BEDROOM UNITS            EACH    $40,010         $680,171

GROSS LOW INCOME SALES PROCEEDS                     $1,940,432
    LESS SALES EXPENSE                    3.0%          $58,809
    LESS PRO RATA DEVELOPMENT COSTS                  $7,864,819
    LESS RETURN ON SALES                 15.0%         $691,065
NET PROFIT (GAP) AFTER SALES ==================)    ($5,474,250)

            SALES PRICE/NSF 2 BEDROOMS:    $43.61
            SALES PRICE/NSF 3 BEDROOMS:    $37.81
------------------------------------------------------------

GAP ANALYSIS.

PROFIT (GAP) FROM MARKET RATE SALES                   $701,3

    1 BEDROOM UNITS·          PER UNIT    $11,261)      $335,279)
    2 BEDROOM UNITS.          PER UNIT    $16,230       $405,740)

PROFIT (GAP) FROM MODERATE INCOME SALES              $4,401,163)

    2 BEDROOM UNITS·          PER UNIT    $81,664)    $2,775,214)
    3 BEDROOM UNITS:          PER UNIT    $101,622)   $1,625,343)

PROFIT GAP) FROM LOW INCOME SALES                    $5,474,250)

    2 BEDROOM UNITS·          PER UNIT    $99,224     $3,373,356)
    3 BEDROOM UNITS:          PER UNIT   ($120,547)   $2,100,294)

                                                    -----------
TOTAL PROFIT (GAP) AFTER SALES -------------------)  $10,576,542)
```

SOUTH END NEIGHBORHOOD HOUSING INITIATIVE
        PARCEL NUMBER: AGGREGATE OF ALL PHASE 1B VACANT LOTS (#9 - 15)
        PARCEL DESCRIPTION: R11-C, RE-7B, 29-A, R-12A, R-12B, 33B, SE-98A.

PREPARED BY THE BOSTON REDEVELOPMENT AUTHORITY
==

DEVELOPMENT PROGRAM:		
BUILDING SIZE	152,285	
PARCEL SIZE	76,360 SF	
NUMBER OF UNITS	152 UNITS	
PARKING SPACES	106 SPACES	
EQUITY REQUIREMENT	15% OF TDC	

==

UNIT MIX:

MARKET RATE	33.0%	(NO INCOME LIMIT)
MODERATE INCOME	33.0%	(NOT MORE THAN 80% OF SMSA MEDIAN INCOME)
LOW INCOME	33.0%	(NOT MORE THAN 50% OF SMSA MEDIAN INCOME)

==

UNIT COMPOSITION:	NO. UNITS	% AGE	GSF	NSF	EFFICIENCY
MARKET RATE					
1 BEDROOM UNITS	26	50%	700	595	85.0%
2 BEDROOM UNITS	25	50%	1,000	850	85.0%
TOTAL MARKET RATE UNITS	51	100%	43,200	36,720	85.0%
MODERATE INCOME					
2 BEDROOM UNITS	34	67%	1,000	850	85.0%
3 BEDROOM UNITS	16	33%	1,245	1,058	85.0%
TOTAL MODERATE RATE UNITS	50	100%	53,920	45,832	85.0%
LOW INCOME					
2 BEDROOM UNITS	34	67%	1,000	850	85.0%
3 BEDROOM UNITS	17	33%	1,245	1,058	85.0%
TOTAL LOW INCOME UNITS	51	100%	55,165	46,890	85.0%
GRAND TOTAL	152		152,285	129,442	

==

DEVELOPMENT PRO FORMA

	UNIT COST	TOTAL COST
LAND COST:	===========	============
MARKET RATE UNITS	$25,000 /DU (FRV)	$1,275,000
MODERATE INCOME UNITS	$10,000 /DU (FRV)	$500,000
LOW INCOME UNITS	$5,000 /DU (FRV)	$255,000
TOTAL LAND COST --------------------------------------)		$2,030,000
HARD COSTS		
RESIDENTIAL CONSTRUCTION	$90 PER GSF	$13,705,650
TOTAL HARD COSTS (HC) -------------------------------)		$13,705,650
PROJECT-RELATED SOFT COSTS:		
A/E FEE	6.0% OF HC	$822,339
LEGAL FEES	3.0% OF HC	$411,170
ACCOUNTING FEES	0.4% OF HC	$54,823
DEVELOPER'S FEE	4.0% OF HC	$548,226
TRESOR FEES (LOW/MOD UNITS ONLY)	$500 PER UNIT	$50,500
RE TAXES DURING CONSTRUCTION		$105,991
INSURANCE, TITLE, PERMITS	1.00% OF HC	$137,057
MARKETING (MKT RATE UNITS)	$600 PER UNIT	$30,600
PROCESSING FEES (LOW/MOD UNITS)	$0 PER UNIT	$0
CONDO CARRYING COSTS (MKT UNITS)	10.00% PER YEAR	$215,760
CONSTRUCTION INTEREST	10.00% PER YEAR	$766,591
TOTAL SOFT COSTS (SC) --------------------------)		$3,136,369
TOTAL PROJECT COSTS		$18,872,619
CONTINGENCY (% HARD COSTS)	5.0%	$685,283
TOTAL DEVELOPMENT COST =========================)		$19,557,902
EQUITY REQUIREMENT		$2,933,685
TDC/GSF		$128.43
TDC/1 BEDROOM UNIT		$89,901
TDC/2 BEDROOM UNIT		$128,430
TDC/3 BEDROOM UNIT		$159,895

CASE   Ib
MKT   33.0%
MOD   33.0%
LOW   33.0%
NON PROFIT IF 1   0
BMR LAND IF 1   0
HOP IF 1   1
NO LAND COST IF 0   1
PTNRSHP IF 1   0
NO EQUITY IF 0   1
MKT PRICE/NSF $165
EFFICIENCY   85.0%

```
NEW CONSTRUCTION ANALYSIS      PERCENT MARKET RATE:        33.3%
PARCELS NUMBER 9 THRU 15       PERCENT MOD INCOME:         33.0%
OWNERSHIP SCENARIO:            PERCENT LOW INCOME:         33.0%
===============================================================

MARKET RATE SALES         PRICE/NSF =        $165

    1 BEDROOM UNITS          EACH    $98,175      $2,552,550
    2 BEDROOM UNITS          EACH   $140,250      $3,506,250

GROSS SALES PROCEEDS OF MARKET RATE UNITS         $6,058,800
    LESS SALES EXPENSE                    5.0%       $302,940
    LESS PRO RATA DEVELOPMENT COSTS                $5,548,159
    LESS RETURN ON SALES                15.0%       $908,820
NET PROFIT (GAP) AFTER SALES ==================)   ($701,119)

---------------------------------------------------------------
MODERATE INCOME SALES (80% OF MEDIAN INCOME)
    MAX ANNUAL MTG PAYMENT (FAM OF 4):   $5,440  (20% OF INCOME)
    MAX ANNUAL MTG PAYMENT (FAM OF 5):   $5,872  (20% OF INCOME)
            MORTGAGE INTERTEST RATE:      5.50%
    DOWN PAYMENT PERCENT OF SALES PRICE:  5.00%
MAXIMUM SALES PRICE MODERATE INCOME:
    2 BEDROOM UNITS          EACH    $84,044      $2,857,498
    3 BEDROOM UNITS          EACH    $90,718      $1,451,491

GROSS MODERATE INCOME SALES PROCEEDS              $4,308,989
    LESS SALES EXPENSE                    2.0%        $86,180
    LESS PRO RATA DEVELOPMENT COSTS                $6,924,924
    LESS RETURN ON SALES                15.0%       $646,348
NET PROFIT (GAP) AFTER SALES ==================)  ($3,348,463)

            SALES PRICE/NSF 2 BEDROOMS:   $78.88
            SALES PRICE/NSF 3 BEDROOMS:   $85.72

---------------------------------------------------------------
LOW INCOME SALES (50% OF MEDIAN INCOME):
    MAX ANNUAL MTG PAYMENT (FAM OF 4):   $3,410  (20% OF INCOME)
    MAX ANNUAL MTG PAYMENT (FAM OF 5):   $3,670  (20% OF INCOME)
            INTEREST RATE:                5.50%
    DOWNPAYMENT PERCENT OF SALES PRICE:   5.00%
MAXIMUM SALES PRICE LOW INCOME:
    2 BEDROOM UNITS          EACH    $52,528      $1,785,936
    3 BEDROOM UNITS          EACH    $56,639        $962,880

GROSS LOW INCOME SALES PROCEEDS                   $2,749,817
    LESS SALES EXPENSE                    2.0%        $54,996
    LESS PRO RATA DEVELOPMENT COSTS                $7,084,819
    LESS RETURN ON SALES                15.0%       $412,472
NET PROFIT (GAP) AFTER SALES ==================)  ($4,802,471)

            SALES PRICE/NSF 2 BEDROOMS:   $61.80
            SALES PRICE/NSF 3 BEDROOMS:   $53.58

---------------------------------------------------------------
GAP ANALYSIS:

PROFIT (GAP) FROM MARKET RATE SALES                ($701,119)

    1 BEDROOM UNITS:        PER UNIT  ($11,361)     ($295,373)
    2 BEDROOM UNITS:        PER UNIT  ($16,230)      $405,740)

PROFIT (GAP) FROM MODERATE INCOME SALES          ($3,348,463)

    2 BEDROOM UNITS:        PER UNIT   ($62,091)  ($2,111,463)
    3 BEDROOM UNITS:        PER UNIT   ($77,215)  ($1,237,044)

PROFIT (GAP) FROM LOW INCOME SALES               ($4,802,471)

    2 BEDROOM UNITS:        PER UNIT   ($87,563)  ($2,359,920)
    3 BEDROOM UNITS:        PER UNIT  ($108,085)  ($1,842,550)

                                                 -------------
TOTAL PROFIT (GAP) AFTER SALES -------------------)  ($8,852,053)
```

SOUTH END NEIGHBORHOOD HOUSING INITIATIVE
          PARCEL NUMBER: AGGREGATE OF ALL PHASE 1B VACANT LOTS (#9 - 15)
          PARCEL DESCRIPTION: R11-C, RE-7B, 29-A, R-12A, R-12B, 33B, SE-98A.

PREPARED BY THE BOSTON REDEVELOPMENT AUTHORITY

CASE Ic
MKT   33.0%
MOD   33.0%
LOW   33.0%
NON PROFIT IF 1   0
EMR LAND IF 1   1
HOP IF 1   1
NO LAND COST IF 0   1
PTNRSHP IF 1   0
NO EQUITY IF 0   1
MKT PRICE/NSF $165
EFFICIENCY   35.0%

===
DEVELOPMENT PROGRAM:
   BUILDING SIZE   152,285
   PARCEL SIZE   76,360 SF
   NUMBER OF UNITS   152 UNITS
   PARKING SPACES   106 SPACES
   EQUITY REQUIREMENT   15% OF TDC
===

UNIT MIX:

   MARKET RATE   33.0% (NO INCOME LIMIT)
   MODERATE INCOME   33.0% (NOT MORE THAN 80% OF SMSA MEDIAN INCOME)
   LOW INCOME   33.0% (NOT MORE THAN 50% OF SMSA MEDIAN INCOME)
===

UNIT COMPOSITION:	NO. UNITS	% AGE	GSF	NSF	EFFICIENCY
MARKET RATE					
1 BEDROOM UNITS	26	50%	700	595	85.0%
2 BEDROOM UNITS	25	50%	1,000	850	85.0%
TOTAL MARKET RATE UNITS	51	100%	43,200	36,720	85.0%
MODERATE INCOME					
2 BEDROOM UNITS	34	67%	1,000	850	85.0%
3 BEDROOM UNITS	16	33%	1,245	1,058	85.0%
TOTAL MODERATE RATE UNITS	50	100%	53,920	45,832	85.0%
LOW INCOME					
2 BEDROOM UNITS	34	67%	1,000	850	85.0%
3 BEDROOM UNITS	17	33%	1,245	1,058	85.0%
TOTAL LOW INCOME UNITS	51	100%	55,165	46,890	85.0%
GRAND TOTAL	152		152,285	129,442	

===
DEVELOPMENT PRO FORMA

	UNIT COST	TOTAL COST
LAND COST:		
MARKET RATE UNITS	$25,000 /DU (FRV)	$1,275,000
MODERATE INCOME UNITS	$0 /DU (FRV)	$0
LOW INCOME UNITS	$0 /DU (FRV)	$0
TOTAL LAND COST ------------------------)		$1,275,000
HARD COSTS:		
RESIDENTIAL CONSTRUCTION	$90 PER GSF	$13,705,650
TOTAL HARD COSTS (HC) ------------------)		$13,705,630
PROJECT-RELATED SOFT COSTS:		
A/E FEE	6.0% OF HC	$822,339
LEGAL FEES	3.0% OF HC	$411,170
ACCOUNTING FEES	0.4% OF HC	$54,823
DEVELOPER'S FEE	4.0% OF HC	$548,226
TREODR FEES (LOW/MOD UNITS ONLY)	$500 PER UNIT	$50,500
RE TAXES DURING CONSTRUCTION		$100,820
INSURANCE, TITLE, PERMITS	1.00% OF HC	$127,057
MARKETING (MKT RATE UNITS)	$600 PER UNIT	$30,600
PROCESSING FEES (LOW/MOD UNITS)	$0 PER UNIT	$0
CONDO CARRYING COSTS (MKT UNITS)	10.00% PER YEAR	$206,500
CONSTRUCTION INTEREST	10.00% PER YEAR	$729,298
TOTAL SOFT COSTS (SC) ------------------)		$3,090,421
TOTAL PROJECT COSTS		$18,071,071
CONTINGENCY (% HARD COSTS)	5.0%	$685,283
TOTAL DEVELOPMENT COST ================)		$18,756,353
EQUITY REQUIREMENT		$2,813,453
TDC/GSF		$123.17
TDC/1 BEDROOM UNIT		$86,216
TDC/2 BEDROOM UNIT		$123,166
TDC/3 BEDROOM UNIT		$153,342

```
NEW CONSTRUCTION ANALYSIS        PERCENT MARKET RATE.          33.0%
PARCELS NUMBER 9 THRU 15         PERCENT MOD INCOME:           33.0%
OWNERSHIP SCENARIO:              PERCENT LOW INCOME:           33.0%
============================================================================

MARKET RATE SALES           PRICE/NSF =        $165

     1 BEDROOM UNITS             EACH    $98,175         $2,552,550
     2 BEDROOM UNITS             EACH   $140,250         $3,506,250

GROSS SALES PROCEEDS OF MARKET RATE UNITS                $6,058,800
  LESS SALES EXPENSE                          5.0%         $302,940
  LESS PRO RATA DEVELOPMENT COSTS                        $5,320,777
  LESS RETURN ON SALES                       15.0%         $908,820
NET PROFIT (GAP) AFTER SALES ===================)         ($473,737)
----------------------------------------------------------------------------
MODERATE INCOME SALES (80% OF MEDIAN INCOME)
     MAX ANNUAL MTG PAYMENT (FAM OF 4).     $5,440   (20% OF INCOME)
     MAX ANNUAL MTG PAYMENT (FAM OF 5).     $5,872   (20% OF INCOME)
        MORTGAGE INTERTEST RATE.            5.50%
  DOWN PAYMENT PERCENT OF SALES PRICE·      5.00%
MAXIMUM SALES PRICE MODERATE INCOME:
     2 BEDROOM UNITS               EACH   $84,044         $2,957,498
     3 BEDROOM UNITS               EACH   $90,718         $1,451,431

GROSS MODERATE INCOME SALES PROCEEDS                     $4,208,389
  LESS SALES EXPENSE                          2.0%          $86,180
  LESS PRO RATA DEVELOPMENT COSTS                        $6,641,117
  LESS RETURN ON SALES                       15.0%         $646,548
NET PROFIT (GAP) AFTER SALES ===================)       ($3,064,657)

           SALES PRICE/NSF 2 BEDROOMS:      $98.88
           SALES PRICE/NSF 3 BEDROOMS:      $85.72
----------------------------------------------------------------------------
LOW INCOME SALES (50% OF MEDIAN INCOME):
     MAX ANNUAL MTG PAYMENT (FAM OF 4):     $3,400   (20% OF INCOME)
     MAX ANNUAL MTG PAYMENT (FAM OF 5):     $3,670   (20% OF INCOME)
                INTEREST RATE:              5.50%
  DOWNPAYMENT PERCENT OF SALES PRICE·       5.00%
MAXIMUM SALES PRICE LOW INCOME:
     2 BEDROOM UNITS               EACH   $52,528         $1,785,936
     3 BEDROOM UNITS               EACH   $56,639           $963,380

GROSS LOW INCOME SALES PROCEEDS                          $2,749,817
  LESS SALES EXPENSE                          2.0%          $54,396
  LESS PRO RATA DEVELOPMENT COSTS                        $6,794,459
  LESS RETURN ON SALES                       15.0%         $412,472
NET PROFIT (GAP) AFTER SALES ===================)       ($4,512,111)

           SALES PRICE/NSF 2 BEDROOMS:      $61.80
           SALES PRICE/NSF 3 BEDROOMS:      $53.58
----------------------------------------------------------------------------
GAP ANALYSIS:

PROFIT (GAP) FROM MARKET RATE SALES                       ($473,737)

     1 BEDROOM UNITS·            PER UNIT    ($7,676)       ($199,583)
     2 BEDROOM UNITS:            PER UNIT   $10,966)        ($274,155)

PROFIT (GAP) FROM MODERATE INCOME SALES                  ($3,064,657)

     2 BEDROOM UNITS·            PER UNIT   ($56,337)      ($1,932,462)
     3 BEDROOM UNITS·            PER UNIT   ($70,762)      ($1,132,195)

PROFIT (GAP) FROM LOW INCOME SALES                       ($4,512,111)

     2 BEDROOM UNITS:            PER UNIT   ($81,790)      ($2,780,962)
     3 BEDROOM UNITS·            PER UNIT  ($101,832)      ($1,731,149)

TOTAL PROFIT (GAP) AFTER SALES -----------------)        ($8,050,505)
```

SOUTH END NEIGHBORHOOD HOUSING INITIATIVE
PARCEL NUMBER: AGGREGATE OF ALL PHASE 1B VACANT LOTS (#9 - 15)
PARCEL DESCRIPTION: R11-C, RE-7B, 29-A, R-12A, R-12B, 33B, SE-98A.

PREPARED BY THE BOSTON REDEVELOPMENT AUTHORITY

CASE	Id	
MKT		65.0%
MOD		17.5%
LOW		17.5%
NON PROFIT IF 1		0
BMR LAND IF 1		1
HOP IF 1		1
NO LAND COST IF 0		1
PTNRSHP IF 1		0
NO EQUITY IF 0		1
MKT PRICE/NSF		$165
EFFICIENCY		85.0%

DEVELOPMENT PROGRAM:
BUILDING SIZE	141,710
PARCEL SIZE	76,360 SF
NUMBER OF UNITS	152 UNITS
PARKING SPACES	106 SPACES
EQUITY REQUIREMENT	15% OF TDC

UNIT MIX:

MARKET RATE	65.0%	(NO INCOME LIMIT)
MODERATE INCOME	17.5%	(NOT MORE THAN 80% OF SMSA MEDIAN INCOME)
LOW INCOME	17.5%	(NOT MORE THAN 50% OF SMSA MEDIAN INCOME)

UNIT COMPOSITION:	NO. UNITS	% AGE	GSF	NSF	EFFICIENCY
MARKET RATE					
1 BEDROOM UNITS	49	50%	700	595	85.0%
2 BEDROOM UNITS	49	50%	1,000	850	85.0%
TOTAL MARKET RATE UNITS	98	100%	83,300	70,805	85.0%
MODERATE INCOME					
2 BEDROOM UNITS	18	67%	1,000	850	85.0%
3 BEDROOM UNITS	9	33%	1,245	1,058	85.0%
TOTAL MODERATE RATE UNITS	27	100%	29,205	24,824	85.0%
LOW INCOME					
2 BEDROOM UNITS	18	67%	1,000	850	85.0%
3 BEDROOM UNITS	9	33%	1,245	1,058	85.0%
TOTAL LOW INCOME UNITS	27	100%	29,205	24,824	85.0%
GRAND TOTAL	152		141,710	120,454	

DEVELOPMENT PRO FORMA

	UNIT COST	TOTAL COST
LAND COST:		
MARKET RATE UNITS	$25,000 /DU (FMV)	$2,450,000
MODERATE INCOME UNITS	$0 /DU (FMV)	$0
LOW INCOME UNITS	$0 /DU (FMV)	$0
TOTAL LAND COST ----------------------)		$2,450,000
HARD COSTS:		
RESIDENTIAL CONSTRUCTION	$90 PER GSF	$12,753,900
TOTAL HARD COSTS (HC) ----------------)		$12,753,900
PROJECT-RELATED SOFT COSTS:		
A/E FEE	6.0% OF HC	$765,234
LEGAL FEES	3.0% OF HC	$382,617
ACCOUNTING FEES	0.4% OF HC	$51,016
DEVELOPER'S FEE	4.0% OF HC	$510,156
RESDR FEES (LOW/MOD UNITS ONLY)	$500 PER UNIT	$27,000
RE TAXES DURING CONSTRUCTION		$108,322
INSURANCE, TITLE, PERMITS	1.00% OF HC	$127,539
MARKETING (MKT RATE UNITS)	$600 PER UNIT	$58,800
PROCESSING FEES (LOW/MOD UNITS)	$0 PER UNIT	$0
CONDO CARRYING COSTS (MKT UNITS)	10.00% PER YEAR	$430,411
CONSTRUCTION INTEREST	10.00% PER YEAR	$732,215
TOTAL SOFT COSTS (SC) ----------------)		$3,187,309
TOTAL PROJECT COSTS		$18,391,209
CONTINGENCY (% HARD COSTS)	5.0%	$637,695
TOTAL DEVELOPMENT COST ===============)		$19,028,904
EQUITY REQUIREMENT		$2,854,336
TDC/GSF		$134.28
TDC/1 BEDROOM UNIT		$93,996
TDC/2 BEDROOM UNIT		$134,281
TDC/3 BEDROOM UNIT		$167,179

-47-

```
NEW CONSTRUCTION ANALYSIS      PERCENT MARKET RATE.        65.0%
PARCELS NUMBER 9 THRU 15       PERCENT MOD INCOME:         17.5%
OWNERSHIP SCENARIO:            PERCENT LOW INCOME,         17.5%
================================================================

MARKET RATE SALES          PRICE/NSF =      $165

    1 BEDROOM UNITS            EACH    $98,175     $4,810,575
    2 BEDROOM UNITS            EACH    $140,250    $6,872,250

GROSS SALES PROCEEDS OF MARKET RATE UNITS              $11,682,825
    LESS SALES EXPENSE                        5.0%        $584,141
    LESS PRO RATA DEVELOPMENT COSTS                    $11,185,574
    LESS RETURN ON SALES                     15.0%      $1,752,424
NET PROFIT (GAP) AFTER SALES ==================)       ($1,839,314)
----------------------------------------------------------------
MODERATE INCOME SALES (80% OF MEDIAN INCOME)
    MAX ANNUAL MTG PAYMENT (FAM OF 4):      $5,440   (20% OF INCOME)
    MAX ANNUAL MTG PAYMENT (FAM OF 5).      $5,872   (20% OF INCOME)
              MORTGAGE INTERTEST RATE:      5.50%
    DOWN PAYMENT PERCENT OF SALES PRICE.    5.00%
MAXIMUM SALES PRICE MODERATE INCOME:
    2 BEDROOM UNITS               EACH   $84,044     $1,512,793
    3 BEDROOM UNITS               EACH   $90,718       $816,463
                                                   ------------
GROSS MODERATE INCOME SALES PROCEEDS                   $2,329,257
    LESS SALES EXPENSE                       2.0%        $46,585
    LESS PRO RATA DEVELOPMENT COSTS                    $3,921,665
    LESS RETURN ON SALES                    15.0%       $349,388
NET PROFIT (GAP) AFTER SALES ==================)      ($1,988,382)

            SALES PRICE/NSF 2 BEDROOMS:     $98.88
            SALES PRICE/NSF 3 BEDROOMS:     $85.72
----------------------------------------------------------------
LOW INCOME SALES (50% OF MEDIAN INCOME)
    MAX ANNUAL MTG PAYMENT (FAM OF 4):      $3,400   (20% OF INCOME)
    MAX ANNUAL MTG PAYMENT (FAM OF 5):      $3,670   (20% OF INCOME)
                   INTEREST RATE:           5.50%
    DOWNPAYMENT PERCENT OF SALES PRICE:     5.00%
MAXIMUM SALES PRICE LOW INCOME:
    2 BEDROOM UNITS               EACH   $52,528      $945,436
    3 BEDROOM UNITS               EACH   $56,699      $510,290
                                                   ------------
GROSS LOW INCOME SALES PROCEEDS                        $1,455,785
    LESS SALES EXPENSE                       2.0%        $29,116
    LESS PRO RATA DEVELOPMENT COSTS                    $3,921,665
    LESS RETURN ON SALES                    15.0%       $218,368
NET PROFIT (GAP) AFTER SALES ==================)      ($2,713,363)

            SALES PRICE/NSF 2 BEDROOMS;     $61.80
            SALES PRICE/NSF 3 BEDROOMS.     $53.58
----------------------------------------------------------------
GAP ANALYSIS:

PROFIT (GAP) FROM MARKET RATE SALES                   ($1,839,314)

    1 BEDROOM UNITS:            PER UNIT   ($15,456)    ($757,365)
    2 BEDROOM UNITS:            PER UNIT    ($22,081)  ($1,081,95 )

PROFIT (GAP) FROM MODERATE INCOME SALES                $1,988,362

    2 BEDROOM UNITS:            PER UNIT    $68,84)    ($1,225,5/5)
    3 BEDROOM UNITS:            PER UNIT    ($94,784)    ($762,377)

PROFIT (GAP) FROM LOW INCOME SALES                     $2,713,363

    2 BEDROOM UNITS:            PER UNIT    ($92,907)  ($1,672,335)
    3 BEDROOM UNITS.            PER UNIT    $115,670)  ($1,041,28)
                                                   ------------
TOTAL PROFIT GAP) AFTER SALES -------------------)    $6,541,159)
```

SOUTH END NEIGHBORHOOD HOUSING INITIATIVE
   PARCEL NUMBER: AGGREGATE OF ALL PHASE 1B VACANT LOTS (#9 - 15)
   PARCEL DESCRIPTION: R11-C, RE-78, 29-A, R-12A, R-12B, 33E, SE-98A.

PREPARED BY THE BOSTON REDEVELOPMENT AUTHORITY
===

DEVELOPMENT PROGRAM:
   BUILDING SIZE   146,970
   PARCEL SIZE   76,360 SF
   NUMBER OF UNITS   152 UNITS
   PARKING SPACES   106 SPACES
   EQUITY REQUIREMENT   15% OF TDC
===

CASE	Ie	
MKT		50.0%
MOD		25.0%
LOW		25.0%
NON PROFIT IF 1		0
BMR LAND IF 1		1
HOP IF 1		1
NO LAND COST IF 0		1
PTNRSHP IF 1		0
NO EQUITY IF 0		1
MKT PRICE/NSF		$165
EFFICIENCY		85.0%

UNIT MIX:

MARKET RATE	50.0%	(NO INCOME LIMIT)
MODERATE INCOME	25.0%	(NOT MORE THAN 80% OF SMSA MEDIAN INCOME)
LOW INCOME	25.0%	(NOT MORE THAN 50% OF SMSA MEDIAN INCOME)

UNIT COMPOSITION:	NO. UNITS	% AGE	GSF	NSF	EFFICIENCY
MARKET RATE					
1 BEDROOM UNITS	38	50%	700	595	85.0%
2 BEDROOM UNITS	38	50%	1,000	850	85.0%
TOTAL MARKET RATE UNITS	76	100%	64,600	54,910	85.0%
MODERATE INCOME					
2 BEDROOM UNITS	25	67%	1,000	850	85.0%
3 BEDROOM UNITS	13	33%	1,245	1,058	85.0%
TOTAL MODERATE RATE UNITS	38	100%	41,185	35,007	85.0%
LOW INCOME					
2 BEDROOM UNITS	25	67%	1,000	850	85.0%
3 BEDROOM UNITS	13	33%	1,245	1,058	85.0%
TOTAL LOW INCOME UNITS	38	100%	41,185	35,007	85.0%
GRAND TOTAL	152		146,970	124,925	

===
DEVELOPMENT PRO FORMA

	UNIT COST	TOTAL COST
LAND COST:		
MARKET RATE UNITS	$25,000 /DU (FRV)	$1,900,000
MODERATE INCOME UNITS	$0 /DU (FRV)	$0
LOW INCOME UNITS	$0 /DU (FRV)	$0
TOTAL LAND COST ----------------------------)		$1,900,000
HARD COSTS		
RESIDENTIAL CONSTRUCTION	$90 PER GSF	$13,227,000
TOTAL HARD COSTS (HC) ----------------------)		$13,227,000
PROJECT-RELATED SOFT COSTS:		
A/E FEE	6.0% OF HC	$793,620
LEGAL FEES	2.0% OF HC	$396,810
ACCOUNTING FEES	1.4% OF HC	$562,849
DEVELOPER'S FEE	4.0% OF HC	$529,458
REGOR FEES (LOW/MOD UNITS ONLY)	$500 PER UNIT	$28,000
RE TAXES DURING CONSTRUCTION		$191,307
INSURANCE, TITLE, PERMITS	1.00% OF HC	$132,273
MARKETING (MKT RATE UNITS)	$600 PER UNIT	$45,600
PROCESSING FEES (LOW/MOD UNITS)	$0 PER UNIT	$0
CONDO CARRYING COSTS (MKT UNITS)	10 N % PER YEAR	$28',6?+
CONSTRUCTION INTEREST	10.00% PER YEAR	$511,141
TOTAL SOFT COSTS (SC) -----------------------)		$3,140,515
TOTAL PROJECT COSTS		$18,270,915
CONTINGENCY (% HARD COSTS)	5.0%	$661,265
TOTAL DEVELOPMENT COST ===================)		$18,902,175
EQUITY REQUIREMENT		$2,833,307
TDC/GSF		$128.82
TDC/1 BEDROOM UNIT		$90,173
TDC/2 BEDROOM UNIT		$128,814
TDC/3 BEDROOM UNIT		$160,177

```
NEW CONSTRUCTION ANALYSIS        PERCENT MARKET RATE.        50. %
PARCELS NUMBER 9 THRU 15         PERCENT MOD INCOME          25 0%
OWNERSHIP SCENARIO:              PERCENT LOW INCOME.         25. 0%
===================================================================

MARKET RATE SALES          PRICE/NSF =      $165

     1 BEDROOM UNITS            EACH    $98,175      $3,730,650
     2 BEDROOM UNITS            EACH   $140,250      $5,329,500
                                                    -----------
GROSS SALES PROCEEDS OF MARKET RATE UNITS           $9,060,150
     LESS SALES EXPENSE                      5.0%     $452,008
     LESS PRO RATA DEVELOPMENT COSTS                $8,321,553
     LESS RETURN ON SALES                   15.0%   $1,359,023
NET PROFIT (GAP) AFTER SALES ===================)   ($1,073,433)

-------------------------------------------------------------------
MODERATE INCOME SALES (80% OF MEDIAN INCOME)
     MAX ANNUAL MTG PAYMENT (FAM OF 4):   $5,440  (20% OF INCOME)
     MAX ANNUAL MTG PAYMENT (FAM OF 5):   $5,872  (20% OF INCOME)
              MORTGAGE INTEREST RATE:      5.50%
     DOWN PAYMENT PERCENT OF SALES PRICE.  5.00%
MAXIMUM SALES PRICE MODERATE INCOME:
     2 BEDROOM UNITS            EACH    $84,044      $2,101,102
     3 BEDROOM UNITS            EACH    $90,718      $1,179,336
                                                    -----------
GROSS MODERATE INCOME SALES PROCEEDS                $3,280,438
     LESS SALES EXPENSE                      3.0%      $65,609
     LESS PRO RATA DEVELOPMENT COSTS                $3,305,312
     LESS RETURN ON SALES                   15.0%     $492,066
NET PROFIT (GAP) AFTER SALES ===================)   ($2,582,549)

          SALES PRICE/NSF 2 BEDROOMS:     $88.98
          SALES PRICE/NSF 3 BEDROOMS      $85.72

-------------------------------------------------------------------
LOW INCOME SALES (50% OF MEDIAN INCOME):
     MAX ANNUAL MTG PAYMENT (FAM OF 4):   $3,440  (20% OF INCOME)
     MAX ANNUAL MTG PAYMENT (FAM OF 5):   $3,670  (20% OF INCOME)
                    INTEREST RATE:         5.00%
     DOWN PAYMENT PERCENT OF SALES PRICE:  5.00%
MAXIMUM SALES PRICE LOW INCOME:
     2 BEDROOM UNITS            EACH    $52,505      $1,313,189
     3 BEDROOM UNITS            EACH    $56,599        $737,085
                                                    -----------
GROSS LOW INCOME SALES PROCEEDS                     $2,050,274
     LESS SALES EXPENSE                      3.0%      $4,005
     LESS PRO RATA DEVELOPMENT COSTS                $3,305,312
     LESS RETURN ON SALES                   15.0%     $307,541
NET PROFIT (GAP) AFTER SALES ===================)   ($3,603,585)

          SALES PRICE/NSF 2 BEDROOMS:     $61.30
          SALES PRICE/NSF 3 BEDROOMS      $53.58

----------------------------------------------------------------- --
GAP ANALYSIS.

PROFIT (GAP) FROM MARKET RATE SALES                 ($1,073,433)

     1 BEDROOM UNITS:           PER UNIT   $3,...528    ($446,828)
     2 BEDROOM UNITS.           PER UNIT   $16,067      $601,431

PROFIT (GAP) FROM MODERATE INCOME SALES             ($2,582,549)

     2 BEDROOM UNITS            PER UNIT   $62,706    $1,567,650
     3 BEDROOM UNITS.           PER UNIT   $73,363    $1,014,337

PROFIT (GAP) FROM LOW INCOME SALES                  ($3,603,585)

     2 BEDROOM UNITS:           PER UNIT   $87,493    $2,187,423
     3 BEDROOM UNITS:           PER UNIT   $,8,324    $1,416,147
                                                    -----------
TOTAL PROFIT (GAP) AFTER SALES ------- ----------)  ($7,053,567)
```

SOUTH END NEIGHBORHOOD HOUSING INITIATIVE
PARCEL NUMBER: AGGREGATE OF ALL PHASE 1B VACANT LOTS (#9 - 15)
PARCEL DESCRIPTION: R11-C, RE-7B, 29-A, R-12A, R-12B, 339, SE-98A.

PREPARED BY THE BOSTON REDEVELOPMENT AUTHORITY
===

CASE   IIA
MKT   33.0%
MOD   33.0%
LOW   33.0%
NON PROFIT IF 1   1
BMR LAND IF 1   0
HOP IF 1   0
NO LAND COST IF 0   1
PTNRSHP IF 1   0
NO EQUITY IF 0   1
MKT PRICE/NSF $165
EFFICIENCY   85.0%

DEVELOPMENT PROGRAM:
BUILDING SIZE   152,285
PARCEL SIZE   76,360 SF
NUMBER OF UNITS   152 UNITS
PARKING SPACES   106 SPACES
EQUITY REQUIREMENT   5% OF TDC
===

UNIT MIX:

MARKET RATE   33.0%   (NO INCOME LIMIT)
MODERATE INCOME   33.0%   (NOT MORE THAN 80% OF SMSA MEDIAN INCOME)
LOW INCOME   33.0%   (NOT MORE THAN 50% OF SMSA MEDIAN INCOME)
===

UNIT COMPOSITION:	NO. UNITS	% AGE	GSF	NSF	EFFICIENCY
MARKET RATE					
1 BEDROOM UNITS	26	50%	700	595	85.0%
2 BEDROOM UNITS	25	50%	1,000	850	85.0%
TOTAL MARKET RATE UNITS	51	100%	43,200	36,720	85.0%
MODERATE INCOME					
2 BEDROOM UNITS	34	67%	1,000	850	85.0%
3 BEDROOM UNITS	16	33%	1,245	1,058	85.0%
TOTAL MODERATE RATE UNITS	50	100%	53,900	45,832	85.0%
LOW INCOME					
2 BEDROOM UNITS	34	67%	1,000	850	85.0%
3 BEDROOM UNITS	17	33%	1,245	1,058	85.0%
TOTAL LOW INCOME UNITS	51	100%	55,165	46,890	85.0%
GRAND TOTAL	152		152,285	129,442	

===
DEVELOPMENT PRO FORMA

	UNIT COST	TOTAL COST
LAND COST:		
MARKET RATE UNITS	$25,000 /DU (FRV)	$1,275,000
MODERATE INCOME UNITS	$10,000 /DU (FRV)	$500,000
LOW INCOME UNITS	$5,000 /DU (FRV)	$255,000
TOTAL LAND COST ----------------------)		$2,030,000
HARD COSTS:		
RESIDENTIAL CONSTRUCTION	$90 PER GSF	$13,705,650
TOTAL HARD COSTS (HC) ----------------------)		$13,705,650
PROJECT-RELATED SOFT COSTS:		
A/E FEE	4.0% OF HC	$548,226
LEGAL FEES	1.5% OF HC	$205,585
ACCOUNTING FEES	0.2% OF HC	$27,411
DEVELOPER'S FEE	4.0% OF HC	$548,226
PROCESSOR FEES (LOW/MOD UNITS ONLY)	$500 PER UNIT	$15,500
RE TAXES DURING CONSTRUCTION		$105,301
INSURANCE, TITLE, PERMITS	1.00% OF HC	$137,057
MARKETING (MKT RATE UNITS)	$600 PER UNIT	$30,600
PROCESSING FEES (LOW/MOD UNITS)	$0 PER UNIT	$0
CONDO CARRYING COSTS (MKT UNITS)	10.00% PER YEAR	$204,314
CONSTRUCTION INTEREST	10.00% PER YEAR	$825,385
TOTAL SOFT COSTS (SC) ----------------------)		$2,710,305
TOTAL PROJECT COSTS		$18,443,455
CONTINGENCY (% HARD COSTS)	5.0%	$685,283
TOTAL DEVELOPMENT COST ===================)		$19,104,737
EQUITY REQUIREMENT		$956,737
TDC/GSF		$125.65
TDC/1 BEDROOM UNIT		$87,956
TDC/2 BEDROOM UNIT		$125,651
TDC/3 BEDROOM UNIT		$156,425

```
NEW CONSTRUCTION ANALYSIS    PERCENT MARKET RATE:        33.0%
PARCELS NUMBER 9 THRU 15     PERCENT MOD INCOME:         33.0%
OWNERSHIP SCENARIO.          PERCENT LOW INCOME:         33.0%
=============================================================

MARKET RATE SALES        PRICE/NSF =     $165

   1 BEDROOM UNITS           EACH    $98,175     $2,552,550
   2 BEDROOM UNITS           EACH    $140,250    $3,506,250

GROSS SALES PROCEEDS OF MARKET RATE UNITS         $6,058,800
   LESS SALES EXPENSE                  5.0%         $302,940
   LESS PRO RATA DEVELOPMENT COSTS                $5,428,116
   LESS RETURN ON SALES                0.0%              $0
NET PROFIT (GAP) AFTER SALES ===================)   $327,744

----------------------------------------------------------
MODERATE INCOME SALES (80% OF MEDIAN INCOME)
   MAX ANNUAL MTG PAYMENT (FAM OF 4):  $5,440  (20% OF INCOME)
   MAX ANNUAL MTG PAYMENT (FAM OF 5):  $5,872  (20% OF INCOME)
             MORTGAGE INTEREST RATE.   9.00%
   DOWN PAYMENT PERCENT OF SALES PRICE. 5.00%
MAXIMUM SALES PRICE MODERATE INCOME.
   2 BEDROOM UNITS           EACH     $59,306    $2,016,419
   3 BEDROOM UNITS           EACH     $64,016    $1,024,257

GROSS MODERATE INCOME SALES PROCEEDS              $3,040,676
   LESS SALES EXPENSE                  2.0%          $60,814
   LESS PRO RATA DEVELOPMENT COSTS                $6,775,093
   LESS RETURN ON SALES                0.0%              $0
NET PROFIT (GAP) AFTER SALES ===================)  ($3,795,231)

        SALES PRICE/NSF 2 BEDROOMS:    $69.77
        SALES PRICE/NSF 3 BEDROOMS:    $60.49

----------------------------------------------------------
LOW INCOME SALES (50% OF MEDIAN INCOME):
   MAX ANNUAL MTG PAYMENT (FAM OF 4):  $3,400  (20% OF INCOME)
   MAX ANNUAL MTG PAYMENT (FAM OF 5).  $3,670  (20% OF INCOME)
             INTEREST RATE:            9.00%
   DOWNPAYMENT PERCENT OF SALES PRICE.  5.00%
MAXIMUM SALES PRICE LOW INCOME:
   2 BEDROOM UNITS           EACH     $37,067    $1,260,262
   3 BEDROOM UNITS           EACH     $40,010      $680,171

GROSS LOW INCOME SALES PROCEEDS                   $1,940,432
   LESS SALES EXPENSE                  2.0%          $38,809
   LESS PRO RATA DEVELOPMENT COSTS                $6,331,528
   LESS RETURN ON SALES                0.0%              $0
NET PROFIT (GAP) AFTER SALES ===================)  ($5,029,904)

        SALES PRICE/NSF 2 BEDROOMS:    $43.61
        SALES PRICE/NSF 3 BEDROOMS:    $37.81

----------------------------------------------------------
GAP ANALYSIS:

PROFIT (GAP) FROM MARKET RATE SALES                $327,744

   1 BEDROOM UNITS:          PER UNIT     $5,311     $138,077
   2 BEDROOM UNITS:          PER UNIT     $7,587     $189,667

PROFIT (GAP) FROM MODERATE INCOME SALES           ($3,795,231)

   2 BEDROOM UNITS:          PER UNIT  ($70,086)  ($2,393,135)
   3 BEDROOM UNITS:          PER UNIT  ($87,631)  ($1,402,096)

PROFIT (GAP) FROM LOW INCOME SALES                ($5,029,904)

   2 BEDROOM UNITS.          PER UNIT   ($91,179)  ($3,100,095)
   3 BEDROOM UNITS:          PER UNIT  ($112,513)  ($1,929,803)

                                                  -----------
TOTAL PROFIT (GAP) AFTER SALES ------------------) ($8,437,391)
```

SOUTH END NEIGHBORHOOD HOUSING INITIATIVE
        PARCEL NUMBER: AGGREGATE OF ALL PHASE 1B VACANT LOTS (#9 - 15)
        PARCEL DESCRIPTION: R11-C, RE-7B, 29-A, R-12A, R-12B, 33B, SE-98A.

PREPARED BY THE BOSTON REDEVELOPMENT AUTHORITY
===

		CASE IIb	
		MKT	33.0%
		MOD	33.0%
		LOW	33.0%
		NON PROFIT IF 1	1
		BMR LAND IF 1	0
		HOP IF 1	0
		NO LAND COST IF 0	1
		PTNRSHP IF 1	0
		NO EQUITY IF 0	1
		MKT PRICE/NSF	$165
		EFFICIENCY	85.0%

DEVELOPMENT PROGRAM:
   BUILDING SIZE   152,285
   PARCEL SIZE   76,560 SF
   NUMBER OF UNITS   152 UNITS
   PARKING SPACES   106 SPACES
   EQUITY REQUIREMENT   5% OF TDC
===

UNIT MIX:

   MARKET RATE   33.0% (NO INCOME LIMIT)
   MODERATE INCOME   33.0% (NOT MORE THAN 80% OF SMSA MEDIAN INCOME)
   LOW INCOME   33.0% (NOT MORE THAN 50% OF SMSA MEDIAN INCOME)
===

UNIT COMPOSITION:	NO. UNITS	% AGE	GSF	NSF	EFFICIENCY
MARKET RATE					
1 BEDROOM UNITS	26	50%	700	595	85.0%
2 BEDROOM UNITS	25	50%	1,000	850	85.0%
TOTAL MARKET RATE UNITS	51	100%	43,200	36,720	85.0%
MODERATE INCOME					
2 BEDROOM UNITS	34	67%	1,000	850	85.0%
3 BEDROOM UNITS	16	33%	1,245	1,058	85.0%
TOTAL MODERATE RATE UNITS	50	100%	53,920	45,832	85.0%
LOW INCOME					
2 BEDROOM UNITS	34	67%	1,000	850	85.0%
3 BEDROOM UNITS	17	33%	1,245	1,058	85.0%
TOTAL LOW INCOME UNITS	51	100%	55,165	46,890	85.0%
GRAND TOTAL	152		152,285	129,442	

===
DEVELOPMENT PRO FORMA

	UNIT COST	TOTAL COST
LAND COST:		
MARKET RATE UNITS	$25,000 /DU (FMV)	$1,275,000
MODERATE INCOME UNITS	$10,000 /DU (FMV)	$500,000
LOW INCOME UNITS	$5,000 /DU (FMV)	$255,000
TOTAL LAND COST -------------------------------)		$2,030,000

HARD COSTS:
   RESIDENTIAL CONSTRUCTION $90 PER GSF $13,705,650

TOTAL HARD COSTS (HC) ---------------------------- $13,705,650

PROJECT-RELATED SOFT COSTS:
   A/E FEE   4.0% OF HC $548,226
   LEGAL FEES   1.5% OF HC $205,835
   ACCOUNTING FEES   0.0% OF HC $5,741
   DEVELOPER'S FEE   4.0% OF HC $548,226
   FRESOR FEES (LOW/MOD UNITS ONLY) $500 PER UNIT $50,500
   RE TAXES DURING CONSTRUCTION $2,45,30,
   INSURANCE, TITLE, PERMITS   1.0% OF HC $137,057
   MARKETING (MKT RATE UNITS) $600 PER UNIT $30,600
   PROCESSING FEES (LOW/MOD UNITS) $0 PER UNIT $0
   CONDO CARRYING COSTS (MKT UNITS) 1.0% PER YEAR $214,214
   CONSTRUCTION INTEREST   9.0% PER EAR $962,585

TOTAL SOFT COSTS (SC) ---------------------------- $2,700,315

TOTAL PROJECT COSTS $13,443,455

CONTINGENCY (% HARD COSTS)   5.0% $685,282

TOTAL DEVELOPMENT COST ========================) $13,124,737

EQUITY REQUIREMENT $956,737

TDC/GSF $25.45

TDC/1 BEDROOM UNIT $87,958
TDC/2 BEDROOM UNIT $125,651
TDC/3 BEDROOM UNIT $156,435

                        - 53 -

```
NEW CONSTRUCTION ANALYSIS       PERCENT MARKET RATE:          33.0%
PARCELS NUMBER 9 THRU 15        PERCENT MOD INCOME:           33.0%
OWNERSHIP SCENARIO:             PERCENT LOW INCOME            33.0%
======================================================================

MARKET RATE SALES          PRICE/NSF =      $165

     1 BEDROOM UNITS            EACH     $38,175      $2,552,550
     2 BEDROOM UNITS            EACH     $140,250     $3,506,250

GROSS SALES PROCEEDS OF MARKET RATE UNITS              $6,058,800
  LESS SALES EXPENSE                        5.0%         $302,940
  LESS PRO RATA DEVELOPMENT COSTS                      $5,428,116
  LESS RETURN ON SALES                      0.0%               $0
NET PROFIT (GAP) AFTER SALES ===================)        $327,744
----------------------------------------------------------------------
MODERATE INCOME SALES (80% OF MEDIAN INCOME)
  MAX ANNUAL MTG PAYMENT (FAM OF 4):      $5,440   (20% OF INCOME)
  MAX ANNUAL MTG PAYMENT (FAM OF 5):      $5,872   (20% OF INCOME)
          MORTGAGE INTERTEST RATE:         5.50%
  DOWN PAYMENT PERCENT OF SALES PRICE:     5.00%
MAXIMUM SALES PRICE MODERATE INCOME:
     2 BEDROOM UNITS            EACH     $84,044      $2,857,438
     3 BEDROOM UNITS            EACH     $90,718      $1,451,451

GROSS MODERATE INCOME SALES PROCEEDS                   $4,308,989
  LESS SALES EXPENSE                        2.0%          $86,180
  LESS PRO RATA DEVELOPMENT COSTS                      $6,775,093
  LESS RETURN ON SALES                      0.0%               $0
NET PROFIT (GAP) AFTER SALES ===================)     ($2,552,284)

          SALES PRICE/NSF 2 BEDROOMS.       $98.98
          SALES PRICE/NSF 3 BEDROOMS.       $85.72
----------------------------------------------------------------------
LOW INCOME SALES (50% OF MEDIAN INCOME)
  MAX ANNUAL MTG PAYMENT (FAM OF 4):      $3,400   (20% OF INCOME)
  MAX ANNUAL MTG PAYMENT (FAM OF 5):      $3,670   (20% OF INCOME)
              INTEREST RATE:                5.5%
  DOWNPAYMENT PERCENT OF SALES PRICE:      5.00%
MAXIMUM SALES PRICE LOW INCOME:
     2 BEDROOM UNITS            EACH     $52,528      $1,785,936
     3 BEDROOM UNITS            EACH     $56,633        $362,880

GROSS LOW INCOME SALES PROCEEDS                        $2,748,817
  LESS SALES EXPENSE                        2.0%          $54,996
  LESS PRO RATA DEVELOPMENT COSTS                      $6,901,503
  LESS RETURN ON SALES                      0.0%               $0
NET PROFIT (GAP) AFTER SALES ===================)     ($4,206,719)

          SALES PRICE/NSF 2 BEDROOMS:       $61.80
          SALES PRICE/NSF 3 BEDROOMS:       $53.58
----------------------------------------------------------------------
GAP ANALYSIS.

PROFIT (GAP) FROM MARKET RATE SALES                     $327,744

     1 BEDROOM UNITS:          PER UNIT     $5,311      $128,077
     2 BEDROOM UNITS.          PER UNIT     $7,587      $199,667

PROFIT (GAP) FROM MODERATE INCOME SALES              ($2,552,284)

     2 BEDROOM UNITS:          PER UNIT    ($7,225)   ($1,609,978)
     3 BEDROOM UNITS:          PER UNIT    ($58,902)    ($942,306)

PROFIT (GAP) FROM LOW INCOME SALES                   ($4,206,718)

     2 BEDROOM UNITS:          PER UNIT    ($75,800)  ($2,511,232)
     3 BEDROOM UNITS:          PER UNIT    ($95,217)  ($1,225,486)

                                                      -----------
TOTAL PROFIT GAP AFTER SALES -------------------)    ($6,461,247)
```

SOUTH END NEIGHBORHOOD HOUSING INITIATIVE
          PARCEL NUMBER: AGGREGATE OF ALL PHASE 1B VACANT LOTS (#9 - 15)
          PARCEL DESCRIPTION: R11-C, RE-7B, 29-A, R-12A, R-12B, 33B, SE-98A

PREPARED BY THE BOSTON REDEVELOPMENT AUTHORITY
===

CASE IIC
MKT   33.0%
MOD   33.0%
LOW   33.0%
NON PROFIT IF 1   1
BMR LAND IF 1   1
HOP IF 1   1
NO LAND COST IF 0   1
PTNRSHP IF 1   0
NO EQUITY IF 0   1
MKT PRICE/NSF $165
EFFICIENCY   85.0%

DEVELOPMENT PROGRAM:
    BUILDING SIZE   152,285
    PARCEL SIZE   76,360 SF
    NUMBER OF UNITS   152 UNITS
    PARKING SPACES   106 SPACES
    EQUITY REQUIREMENT   5% OF TDC
===

UNIT MIX:

    MARKET RATE   33.0% (NO INCOME LIMIT)
    MODERATE INCOME   33.0% (NOT MORE THAN 80% OF SMSA MEDIAN INCOME)
    LOW INCOME   33.0% (NOT MORE THAN 50% OF SMSA MEDIAN INCOME)
===

UNIT COMPOSITION:	NO. UNITS	% AGE	GSF	NSF	EFFICIENCY
MARKET RATE					
1 BEDROOM UNITS	26	50%	700	595	85.0%
2 BEDROOM UNITS	25	50%	1,000	850	85.0%
TOTAL MARKET RATE UNITS	51	100%	43,200	36,720	85.0%
MODERATE INCOME					
2 BEDROOM UNITS	34	67%	1,000	850	85.0%
3 BEDROOM UNITS	16	33%	1,245	1,058	85.0%
TOTAL MODERATE RATE UNITS	50	100%	53,920	45,832	85.0%
LOW INCOME					
2 BEDROOM UNITS	34	67%	1,000	850	85.0%
3 BEDROOM UNITS	17	33%	1,245	1,058	85.0%
TOTAL LOW INCOME UNITS	51	100%	55,165	46,890	85.0%
GRAND TOTAL	152		152,285	129,442	

===
DEVELOPMENT PRO FORMA

	UNIT COST	TOTAL COST
LAND COST:		
MARKET RATE UNITS	$25,000 /DU (FRV)	$1,275,000
MODERATE INCOME UNITS	$0 /DU (FRV)	$0
LOW INCOME UNITS	$0 /DU (FRV)	$0
TOTAL LAND COST ------------------------)		$1,275,000
HARD COSTS:		
RESIDENTIAL CONSTRUCTION	$90 PER GSF	$13,705,650
TOTAL HARD COSTS (HC) ------------------,		$13,705,650
PROJECT-RELATED SOFT COSTS:		
A/E FEE	4.0% OF HC	$548,226
LEGAL FEES	.5% OF HC	$215,595
ACCOUNTING FEES	.1% OF HC	$13,741
DEVELOPER'S FEE	4.0% OF HC	$548,226
FRESDR FEES (LOW/MOD UNITS ONLY)	$500 PER UNIT	$50,500
RE TAXES DURING CONSTRUCTION		$104,560
INSURANCE, TITLE, PERMITS	1.00% OF HC	$137,057
MARKETING MKT RATE UNITS)	$600 PER UNIT	$30,600
PROCESSING FEES (LOW/MOD UNITS)	$1 PER UNIT	$0
CONDO CARRYING COSTS (MKT UNITS)	11 % PER YEAR	$624,170
CONSTRUCTION INTEREST	4.0% PER YEAR	$739,391
TOTAL SOFT COSTS (SC) -----------------------)		$2,662,278
TOTAL PROJECT COSTS		$17,643,068
CONTINGENCY (% HARD COSTS)	5. %	$685,283
TOTAL DEVELOPMENT COST ===========================)		$18,328,310
EQUITY REQUIREMENT		$916,416
TDC/GSF		$120.36
TDC/1 BEDROOM UNIT		$84,249
TDC/2 BEDROOM UNIT		$120,355
TDC/3 BEDROOM UNIT		$149,842

```
NEW CONSTRUCTION ANALYSIS        PERCENT MARKET RATE        33.0%
PARCELS NUMBER 9 THRU 15         PERCENT MOD INCOME.        33.0%
OWNERSHIP SCENARIO:              PERCENT LOW INCOME:        33.0%
================================================================

MARKET RATE SALES          PRICE/NSF =      $165

    1 BEDROOM UNITS           EACH    $98,175      $2,552,550
    2 BEDROOM UNITS           EACH    $140,250     $3,506,250
                                                  -----------
GROSS SALES PROCEEDS OF MARKET RATE UNITS         $6,058,800
    LESS SALES EXPENSE                    5.0%       $302,940
    LESS PRO RATA DEVELOPMENT COSTS                $5,199,350
    LESS RETURN ON SALES                 0.0%             $0
NET PROFIT (GAP) AFTER SALES =====================)  $556,510

----------------------------------------------------------------
MODERATE INCOME SALES (80% OF MEDIAN INCOME)
    MAX ANNUAL MTG PAYMENT (FAM OF 4):   $5,440  (20% OF INCOME)
    MAX ANNUAL MTG PAYMENT (FAM OF 5):   $5,872  (20% OF INCOME)
             MORTGAGE INTEREST RATE:      5.50%
    DOWN PAYMENT PERCENT OF SALES PRICE:  5.00%
MAXIMUM SALES PRICE MODERATE INCOME:
    2 BEDROOM UNITS           EACH    $84,044      $2,957,438
    3 BEDROOM UNITS           EACH    $90,718      $1,451,491
                                                  -----------
GROSS MODERATE INCOME SALES PROCEEDS              $4,308,989
    LESS SALES EXPENSE                   2.0%        $86,180
    LESS PRO RATA DEVELOPMENT COSTS                $6,489,559
    LESS RETURN ON SALES                 0.0%             $0
NET PROFIT (GAP) AFTER SALES =====================) $2,266,750)

        SALES PRICE/NSF 2 BEDROOMS:      $98.88
        SALES PRICE/NSF 3 BEDROOMS:      $85.72

----------------------------------------------------------------
LOW INCOME SALES (50% OF MEDIAN INCOME):
    MAX ANNUAL MTG PAYMENT (FAM OF 4):   $3,400  (20% OF INCOME)
    MAX ANNUAL MTG PAYMENT (FAM OF 5):   $3,670  (20% OF INCOME)
             INTEREST RATE:              5.50%
    DOWNPAYMENT PERCENT OF SALES PRICE:   5.00%
MAXIMUM SALES PRICE LOW INCOME:
    2 BEDROOM UNITS           EACH    $52,528      $1,795,916
    3 BEDROOM UNITS           EACH    $56,599        $903,980
                                                  -----------
GROSS LOW INCOME SALES PROCEEDS                   $2,747,817
    LESS SALES EXPENSE                   2.0%        $54,996
    LESS PRO RATA DEVELOPMENT COSTS                $6,633,401
    LESS RETURN ON SALES                  . %             $0
NET PROFIT (GAP) AFTER SALES =====================) ($3,344,581)

        SALES PRICE/NSF 2 BEDROOMS:      $61.80
        SALES PRICE/NSF 3 BEDROOMS:      $53.58

----------------------------------------------------------------
GAP ANALYSIS:

PROFIT (GAP) FROM MARKET RATE SALES                  $556,510

    1 BEDROOM UNITS.        PER UNIT    $9,018       $234,456
    2 BEDROOM UNITS:        PER UNIT   $12,882       $322,054

PROFIT (GAP) FROM MODERATE INCOME SALES           $2,266,750)

    2 BEDROOM UNITS:        PER UNIT   $42,093)    $1,429,000)
    3 BEDROOM UNITS:        PER UNIT   $52,303)      $837,419)

PROFIT (GAP) FROM LOW INCOME SALES                $3,344,581)

    2 BEDROOM UNITS.        PER UNIT    $7,1505)   $2,431,175)
    3 BEDROOM UNITS.        PER UNIT   $89,041)    $1,513,406)
                                                  -----------
TOTAL PROFIT (GAP) AFTER SALES --------------------)  $5,654,821)
```

SOUTH END NEIGHBORHOOD HOUSING INITIATIVE
           PARCEL NUMBER, AGGREGATE OF ALL PHASE 1B VACANT LOTS (#9 - 15)
           PARCEL DESCRIPTION: A11-C, RE-7B, 29-A, R-12A, R-12B, 33B, SE-98A.

PREPARED BY THE BOSTON REDEVELOPMENT AUTHORITY
==

```
CASE  IId
MKT                65.0%
MOD                17.5%
LOW                17.5%
NON PROFIT IF 1        1
BMR LAND IF 1          1
HOP IF 1               1
NO LAND COST IF 0      1
OTNRSHP IF 1           0
NO EQUITY IF 0         1
MKT PRICE/NSF       $165
EFFICIENCY         85.0%
```

DEVELOPMENT PROGRAM:
   BUILDING SIZE   141,710
   PARCEL SIZE   76,360 SF
   NUMBER OF UNITS   152 UNITS
   PARKING SPACES   106 SPACES
   EQUITY REQUIREMENT   5% OF TDC
==

UNIT MIX:

   MARKET RATE   65.0% (NO INCOME LIMIT)
   MODERATE INCOME   17.5% (NOT MORE THAN 80% OF SMSA MEDIAN INCOME)
   LOW INCOME   17.5% (NOT MORE THAN 50% OF SMSA MEDIAN INCOME)
==

UNIT COMPOSITION:	NO. UNITS	% AGE	GSF	NSF	EFFICIENCY
MARKET RATE					
1 BEDROOM UNITS	49	50%	700	595	85.0%
2 BEDROOM UNITS	49	50%	1,000	850	85.0%
TOTAL MARKET RATE UNITS	98	100%	83,300	70,805	85.0%
MODERATE INCOME					
2 BEDROOM UNITS	18	67%	1,000	850	85.0%
3 BEDROOM UNITS	9	33%	1,245	1,058	85.0%
TOTAL MODERATE RATE UNITS	27	100%	29,205	24,824	85.0%
LOW INCOME					
2 BEDROOM UNITS	18	67%	1,000	850	85.0%
3 BEDROOM UNITS	9	33%	1,245	1,058	85.0%
TOTAL LOW INCOME UNITS	27	100%	29,205	24,824	85.0%
GRAND TOTAL	152		141,710	120,454	

==
DEVELOPMENT PRO FORMA

	UNIT COST	TOTAL COST
LAND COST:		
MARKET RATE UNITS	$25,000 /DU (FRV)	$2,450,000
MODERATE INCOME UNITS	$0 /DU (FRV)	$0
LOW INCOME UNITS	$0 /DU (FRV)	$0
TOTAL LAND COST -------------------------------		$2,450,000
HARD COSTS:		
RESIDENTIAL CONSTRUCTION	$90 PER GSF	$12,753,900
TOTAL HARD COSTS (HC) ----------------------------->		$12,753,900
PROJECT-RELATED SOFT COSTS:		
A/E FEE	4.0% OF HC	$510,156
LEGAL FEES	1.5% OF HC	$191,309
ACCOUNTING FEES	0.2% OF HC	$25,508
DEVELOPER'S FEE	4.0% OF HC	$510,156
RESOR FEES (LOW/MOD UNITS ONLY)	$500 PER UNIT	$27,000
RE TAXES DURING CONSTRUCTION		$102,322
INSURANCE, TITLE, PERMITS	1.00% OF HC	$127,539
MARKETING (MKT RATE UNITS)	$600 PER UNIT	$58,800
PROCESSING FEES (LOW/MOD UNITS)	$0 PER UNIT	$0
CONDO CARRYING COSTS (MKT UNITS)	0.6% PER YEAR	$467,871
CONSTRUCTION INTEREST	11.0% PER YEAR	$795,943
TOTAL SOFT COSTS (SC) ----------------------------,		$2,916,604
TOTAL PROJECT COSTS		$18,120,504
CONTINGENCY (% HARD COSTS)	5.0%	$637,695
TOTAL DEVELOPMENT COST ==========================,		$18,758,199
EQUITY REQUIREMENT		$937,910
TDC/GSF		$101.66
TDC/1 BEDROOM UNIT		$92,165
TDC/2 BEDROOM UNIT		$131,565
TDC/3 BEDROOM UNIT		$163,722

```
NEW CONSTRUCTION ANALYSIS        PERCENT MARKET RATE:        65.0%
PARCELS NUMBER 9 THRU 15         PERCENT MOD INCOME:         17.5%
OWNERSHIP SCENARIO.              PERCENT LOW INCOME.         17.5%
```

```
MARKET RATE SALES          PRICE/NSF =      $165

   1 BEDROOM UNITS              EACH    $98,175     $4,810,575
   2 BEDROOM UNITS              EACH   $140,250     $6,872,250
                                                   -----------
GROSS SALES PROCEEDS OF MARKET RATE UNITS         $11,682,825
   LESS SALES EXPENSE                      5.0%       $584,141
   LESS PRO RATA DEVELOPMENT COSTS                 $10,967,666
   LESS RETURN ON SALES                    0.0%            $0
NET PROFIT (GAP) AFTER SALES ===================)     $131,018
```

```
MODERATE INCOME SALES (80% OF MEDIAN INCOME)
    MAX ANNUAL MTG PAYMENT (FAM OF 4).     $5,440  (20% OF INCOME)
    MAX ANNUAL MTG PAYMENT (FAM OF 5):     $5,872  (20% OF INCOME)
             MORTGAGE INTERTEST RATE:       5.50%
   DOWN PAYMENT PERCENT OF SALES PRICE:     5.00%
MAXIMUM SALES PRICE MODERATE INCOME:
   2 BEDROOM UNITS              EACH    $84,044     $1,512,793
   3 BEDROOM UNITS              EACH    $90,718       $816,463
                                                   -----------
GROSS MODERATE INCOME SALES PROCEEDS               $2,329,257
   LESS SALES EXPENSE                      2.0%        $46,585
   LESS PRO RATA DEVELOPMENT COSTS                  $3,845,266
   LESS RETURN ON SALES                    0.0%            $0
NET PROFIT (GAP) AFTER SALES ==================)  ($1,562,595)

          SALES PRICE/NSF 2 BEDROOMS'      $98.88
          SALES PRICE/NSF 3 BEDROOMS.      $85.72
```

```
LOW INCOME SALES (50% OF MEDIAN INCOME):
    MAX ANNUAL MTG PAYMENT (FAM OF 4):     $3,400  (20% OF INCOME)
    MAX ANNUAL MTG PAYMENT (FAM OF 5):     $3,670  (20% OF INCOME)
                      INTEREST RATE:        5.50%
   DOWNPAYMENT PERCENT OF SALES PRICE:      5.00%
MAXIMUM SALES PRICE LOW INCOME:
   2 BEDROOM UNITS              EACH    $52,528       $945,496
   3 BEDROOM UNITS              EACH    $56,699       $510,290
                                                   -----------
GROSS LOW INCOME SALES PROCEEDS                    $1,455,785
   LESS SALES EXPENSE                      2.0%        $29,116
   LESS PRO RATA DEVELOPMENT COSTS                  $3,845,266
   LESS RETURN ON SALES                    0.0%            $0
NET PROFIT (GAP) AFTER SALES ==================)  ($2,418,597)

          SALES PRICE/NSF 2 BEDROOMS'      $61.80
          SALES PRICE/NSF 3 BEDROOMS:      $53.58
```

```
GAP ANALYSIS.

PROFIT (GAP) FROM MARKET RATE SALES                  $131,018

   1 BEDROOM UNITS.          PER UNIT     $1,101       $53,949
   2 BEDROOM UNITS:          PER UNIT     $1,573       $77,069

PROFIT (GAP) FROM MODERATE INCOME SALES          ($1,562,595)

   2 BEDROOM UNITS:          PER UNIT   ($53,504)    ($963,078)
   3 BEDROOM UNITS.          PER UNIT   ($66,610)    ($599,516)

PROFIT (GAP) FROM LOW INCOME SALES               ($2,418,597)

   2 BEDROOM UNITS.          PER UNIT   ($82,814)  ($1,490,660)
   3 BEDROOM UNITS.          PER UNIT  ($103,104)    ($927,336)
                                                   -----------
TOTAL PROFIT (GAP) AFTER SALES -----------------)  ($3,850,174)
```

SOUTH END NEIGHBORHOOD HOUSING INITIATIVE
        PARCEL NUMBER: AGGREGATE OF ALL PHASE 1B VACANT LOTS (#9 - 15)
        PARCEL DESCRIPTION: R11-C, RE-7B, 29-A, R-12A, R-12B, 33B, SE-98A.

PREPARED BY THE BOSTON REDEVELOPMENT AUTHORITY

CASE IIe
MKT   50.0%
MOD   25.0%
LOW   25.0%
NON PROFIT IF 1   1
BMR LAND IF 1   1
HOP IF 1   1
NO LAND COST IF 0   1
PTNRSHP IF 1   0
NO EQUITY IF 0   1
MKT PRICE/NSF $165
EFFICIENCY   85.0%

DEVELOPMENT PROGRAM:
    BUILDING SIZE   146,970
    PARCEL SIZE   76,360 SF
    NUMBER OF UNITS   152 UNITS
    PARKING SPACES   106 SPACES
    EQUITY REQUIREMENT   5% OF TDC

UNIT MIX.

    MARKET RATE   50.0% (NO INCOME LIMIT)
    MODERATE INCOME   25.0% (NOT MORE THAN 80% OF SMSA MEDIAN INCOME)
    LOW INCOME   25.0% (NOT MORE THAN 50% OF SMSA MEDIAN INCOME)

UNIT COMPOSITION: NO. UNITS   % AGE   GSF   NSF   EFFICIENCY

MARKET RATE
    1 BEDROOM UNITS   38   50%   700   595   85.0%
    2 BEDROOM UNITS   38   50%   1,000   850   85.0%
    TOTAL MARKET RATE UNITS   76   100%   64,500   54,910   85.0%

MODERATE INCOME
    2 BEDROOM UNITS   25   67%   1,000   850   85.0%
    3 BEDROOM UNITS   13   33%   1,245   1,058   85.0%
    TOTAL MODERATE RATE UNITS 38   100%   41,185   35,007   85.0%

LOW INCOME
    2 BEDROOM UNITS   25   67%   1,000   850   85.0%
    3 BEDROOM UNITS   13   33%   1,245   1,058   85.0%
    TOTAL LOW INCOME UNITS   38   100%   41,185   35,007   85.0%

GRAND TOTAL   152   146,970 124,925

DEVELOPMENT PRO FORMA
                            UNIT COST   TOTAL COST
LAND COST:
    MARKET RATE UNITS $25,000 /DU (FRV) $1,900,000
    MODERATE INCOME UNITS $0 /DU (FRV) $0
    LOW INCOME UNITS $0 /DU (FRV) $0

TOTAL LAND COST -----------------------------) $1,900,000

HARD COSTS:
    RESIDENTIAL CONSTRUCTION $90 PER GSF $13,227,300

TOTAL HARD COSTS (HC) --------------------------) $13,227,300

PROJECT-RELATED SOFT COSTS:
    A/E FEE   4.0% OF HC $529,092
    LEGAL FEES   1.5% OF HC $198,410
    ACCOUNTING FEES   0.2% OF HC $26,455
    DEVELOPER'S FEE   4.0% OF HC $529,092
    TREGOR FEES (LOW/MOD UNITS ONLY) $500 PER UNIT $38,000
    RE TAXES DURING CONSTRUCTION $101,807
    INSURANCE, TITLE, PERMITS   1.00% OF HC $132,273
    MARKETING (MKT RATE UNITS) $600 PER UNIT $45,600
    PROCESSING FEES (LOW/MOD UNITS) $0 PER UNIT $0

    CONDO CARRYING COSTS (MKT UNITS) 10.00% PER YEAR $349,255
    CONTRUCTION INTEREST   10.00% PER YEAR $794,581

TOTAL SOFT COSTS (SC) ----------------------------) $2,744,564

TOTAL PROJECT COSTS $17,871,364

CONTINGENCY (% HARD COSTS)   5.0% $661,365

TOTAL DEVELOPMENT COST ===========================) $18,533,229

EQUITY REQUIREMENT $926,661

TDC/GSF $126.10

TDC/1 BEDROOM UNIT $88,271
TDC/2 BEDROOM UNIT $126,102
TDC/3 BEDROOM UNIT $156,997

```
NEW CONSTRUCTION ANALYSIS      PERCENT MARKET RATE:        50.0%
PARCELS NUMBER 9 THRU 15       PERCENT MOD INCOME:         25.0%
OWNERSHIP SCENARIO:            PERCENT LOW INCOME:         25.0%
========================================================================

MARKET RATE SALES           PRICE/NSF =      $165

     1 BEDROOM UNITS            EACH      $98,175     $3,730,650
     2 BEDROOM UNITS            EACH     $140,250     $5,329,500

GROSS SALES PROCEEDS OF MARKET RATE UNITS              $9,060,150
     LESS SALES EXPENSE                     5.0%         $453,008
     LESS PRO RATA DEVELOPMENT COSTS                   $8,146,197
     LESS RETURN ON SALES                   0.0%               $0
NET PROFIT (GAP) AFTER SALES ====================)        $460,945
------------------------------------------------------------------------

MODERATE INCOME SALES (80% OF MEDIAN INCOME)
     MAX ANNUAL MTG PAYMENT (FAM OF 4):    $5,440  (20% OF INCOME)
     MAX ANNUAL MTG PAYMENT (FAM OF 5):    $5,872  (20% OF INCOME)
               MORTGAGE INTERTEST RATE.    5.50%
     DOWN PAYMENT PERCENT OF SALES PRICE:  5.00%
MAXIMUM SALES PRICE MODERATE INCOME:
     2 BEDROOM UNITS            EACH      $84,044     $2,101,102
     3 BEDROOM UNITS            EACH      $90,718     $1,179,336

GROSS MODERATE INCOME SALES PROCEEDS                   $3,280,438
     LESS SALES EXPENSE                     2.0%          $65,609
     LESS PRO RATA DEVELOPMENT COSTS                   $5,193,516
     LESS RETURN ON SALES                   0.0%               $0
NET PROFIT (GAP) AFTER SALES ====================)    ($1,978,687)

          SALES PRICE/NSF 2 BEDROOMS:      $98.88
          SALES PRICE/NSF 3 BEDROOMS:      $85.72
------------------------------------------------------------------------

LOW INCOME SALES (50% OF MEDIAN INCOME).
     MAX ANNUAL MTG PAYMENT (FAM OF 4):    $3,400  (20% OF INCOME)
     MAX ANNUAL MTG PAYMENT (FAM OF 5):    $3,670  (20% OF INCOME)
                    INTEREST RATE·         5.50%
     DOWNPAYMENT PERCENT OF SALES PRICE:   5.00%
MAXIMUM SALES PRICE LOW INCOME:
     2 BEDROOM UNITS            EACH      $52,528     $1,313,189
     3 BEDROOM UNITS            EACH      $56,699       $737,085

GROSS LOW INCOME SALES PROCEEDS                        $2,050,274
     LESS SALES EXPENSE                     2.0%          $41,005
     LESS PRO RATA DEVELOPMENT COSTS                   $5,193,516
     LESS RETURN ON SALES                   0.0%               $0
NET PROFIT (GAP) AFTER SALES ====================)    ($3,184,248)

          SALES PRICE/NSF 2 BEDROOMS:      $61.80
          SALES PRICE/NSF 3 BEDROOMS:      $53.58
------------------------------------------------------------------------

GAP ANALYSIS

PROFIT (GAP) FROM MARKET RATE SALES                      $460,945

     1 BEDROOM UNITS.          PER UNIT     $4,995       $189,801
     2 BEDROOM UNITS:          PER UNIT     $7,135       $271,144

PROFIT (GAP) FROM MODERATE INCOME SALES               ($1,978,687)

     2 BEDROOM UNITS.          PER UNIT  ($48,044)   ($1,201,097)
     3 BEDROOM UNITS:          PER UNIT  ($59,815)     ($777,590)

PROFIT (GAP) FROM LOW INCOME SALES                    ($3,184,248)

     2 BEDROOM UNITS:          PER UNIT  ($77,316)   ($1,932,893)
     3 BEDROOM UNITS:          PER UNIT  ($96,258)   ($1,251,355)
                                                     -----------
TOTAL PROFIT (GAP) AFTER SALES -----------------)    ($4,701,389)
```

GAP ANALYSIS

NEW CONSTRUCTION - 100 RENTAL UNITS

RENTAL ANALYSIS   PHASE 1B   VIGHINI PARCELS 19 - 11
PARCEL DESCRIPTION R11-C, R2-78, 29 & A-120, R 128, 33P
PREPARED BY THE BOSTON REDEVELOPMENT AUTHORITY

MKT/SQFT=0	
SEC 8=0	
SHOP=0	
SUBURBAN=0	
P-SHIP=0	
N/A(HA)=0	
MKT=0	
111C=0	
UNIT RATE	10.5%
MKT	33.0%
MOD	33.0%
LOW	33.0%
DISC RATE	
INFLA FTR	5.0%

DEVELOPMENT PROGRAM:

PARCEL AREA	54,237 GSF
NUMBER OF UNITS	100 UNITS
PARKING SPACES	70 SPACES

| EQUITY REQUIREMENT | 15 0% OF TDC EQUITY |

UNIT MIX

	NO UNITS			
MARKET RATE	33.0%			
MODERATE INCOME	33.0%			
LOW INCOME	33.0%			

UNIT COMPOSITION

	NO UNITS	% AGE	ENO INCOME LIMIT NONE THAN 80% OF SMSA MEDIAN INCOME	GSF	NSF	EFFICIENCY
			NONE THAN 50% OF SMSA MEDIAN INCOME			
MARKET RATE UNITS						
1 BEDROOM UNITS	17	50%		700	595	85.0%
2 BEDROOM UNITS	16	50%		1,000	850	85.0%
TOTAL MARKET RATE UNITS	33	100%		27,900	23,715	85.0%
MODERATE INCOME						
2 BEDROOM UNITS	22	67%		1,000	850	85.0%
3 BEDROOM UNITS	11	33%		1,245	1,058	85.0%
TOTAL MODERATE RATE UNITS	33	100%		25,695	30,341	85.0%
LOW INCOME						
2 BEDROOM UNITS	23	67%		1,000	850	85.0%
3 BEDROOM UNITS	11	33%		1,245	1,058	85.0%
TOTAL LOW INCOME UNITS	34	100%		36,695	31,191	85.0%
TOTAL	100			100,290	85,247	

DEVELOPMENT PRO FORMA:

	UNIT COST	TOTAL COST
LAND COST		
MARKET RATE UNITS	$25,000.00 /BU (FMV)	$825,000
MODERATE INCOME UNITS	$10,000.00 /BU (FMV)	$330,000
LOW INCOME UNITS	$5,000.00 /BU (FMV)	$170,000
TOTAL LAND COST		$1,325,000

HARD COSTS

RESIDENTIAL CONSTRUCTION PER GSF	$90	$9,026,100
TOTAL HARD AND LAND COSTS ---->		$10,351,100

PROJECT RELATED SOFT COSTS

A/E FEE	6.0% OF HC	$541,566
LEGAL FEES	3.0% OF HC	$270,783
ACCOUNTING FEES	0.4% OF HC	$36,104
DEVELOPER'S FEE	4.0% OF HC	$361,044
RE TAXES DURING CONSTRUCTION		$469,643
INSURANCE, TITLE, PERMITS	1.0% OF HC	$90,261
RENT UP AND MARKETING/MARKET	$600 /UNIT	$19,800
RENT-UP AND MARKETING/LOW-MOD	$300 /UNIT	$820,000
RENT-UP DEFICIT	10 0%	$116,428
CONSTRUCTION INTEREST @	10 0%	$904,766
TOTAL SOFT COSTS		$2,030,516
TOTAL PROJECT COSTS		$12,381,616
CONTINGENCY (% OF HARD COSTS)	5.0%	$451,305
TOTAL DEVELOPMENT COST ---->		$12,832,921
EQUITY REQUIREMENT	15 0%	$1,924,938
TDC/GSF		$127 %
TDC/1 BEDROOM UNIT		$86,521
TDC/2 BEDROOM UNIT		$127,958
TDC/3 BEDROOM UNIT		$159,360

-61-

RENTAL INCOME SCHEDULE (YEAR 1, FIRST STABILIZED YEAR)

	Monthly Income/Unit	Yearly Income
TENANT INCOME		
Market Rate Units:		
1 Bedroom	$750	$145,350
2 Bedroom	$1,000	$182,400
Moderate Income Units:		
2 Bedroom	$635	$153,258
3 Bedroom	$683	$165,899
Low Income Units:		
2 Bedroom	$357	$104,093
3 Bedroom	$428	$133,671
TOTAL TENANT INCOME		$736,672

SECTION 8/CHAPTER 707 SUBSIDY INCOME

Low Income:		
2 Bedroom	$0	$0
3 Bedroom	$0	$0
TOTAL SECTION 8/707 INCOME:		

SYNDICATION - TAX CREDIT (10 YEARS)

Low Income:		
2 Bedroom	$407	$112,280 *
3 Bedroom	$419	$55,367 *
TOTAL Syndication		$167,475

SHARP PROGRAM

Moderate Income:		
2 Bedroom	$0	$0
3 Bedroom	$0	$0
Low Income:		
2 Bedroom	$0	$0
3 Bedroom	$0	$0
TOTAL SHARP INCOME:		$0

GAP ANALYSIS (YEAR 1)

ASSUMPTIONS	
OPTION	
MHFA (F-9)	---
SEC 8-9	---
SHARP-9	---
SUBURBAN-9	---
P-SHIP-9	---
MEDIUM-9	---
MHFA-9	---
Irate	10.5%
INFLATION FACTOR	5.0%
OPERATING EXPENSES	($4,379,347)
DEBT SERVICE	($1,197,353)
TENANT INCOME	$736,672
GAP W/O SUBSIDY	($846,031)

GAP FROM ABOVE	($846,031)
SECTION 8 / CHAPTER 707 INCOME	$0
GAP	($846,031)

GAP FROM ABOVE	($846,031)
TAX CREDIT INCOME	$167,475
GAP	($678,556)

EXISTING GAP FROM ABOVE	($678,556)
SHARP INCOME	$0
FINAL BEFORE TAX CASH FLOW	($678,556)
GAP REQUIRED TO BREAK EVEN	($678,556)
GAP INCLUDING A RETURN ON EQUITY OF 15.00%	$582,296

OPERATING PRO FORMA (YEAR 1, FIRST STABILIZED YEAR)

TOTAL INCOME AND SUBSIDIES		
Market Rate Units:		
1 Bedroom	17	$145,350
2 Bedroom	16	$182,400
Moderate Income Units:		
2 Bedroom	22	$153,258
3 Bedroom	11	$165,899
Low Income Units:		
2 Bedroom	23	$216,301
3 Bedroom	11	$168,538
TOTAL INCOME AND SUBSIDIES		$898,146

(See income schedule for specific subsidy breakdown)

EXPENSES:		
Operating Expenses	$3.50 /NSF	($420,363)
Real Estate Taxes	$0.95 /NSF	($80,984)
TOTAL EXPENSES		($379,347)
NET OPERATING INCOME:		$518,799
ANNUAL DEBT SERVICE:		($1,197,353)
Principal $10,907,362		
Interest Rate 10.50%		
Term (Years) 30		
BEFORE TAX CASH FLOW (GAP)		($678,556)

FIFTEEN YEAR OPERATING PRO FORMA   Ia

	1989 1	1990 2	1991 3	1992 4	1993 5	1994 6	1995 7	1996 8	1997 9	1998 10	1999 11	2000 12	2001 13	2002 14	2003 15	2004 16
PROJECT YEAR																
INFLATION/YEAR 5.00%																
INCOME AND SUBSIDIES:																
TOTAL TENANT INCOME:	730,612	767,205	805,565	845,844	888,136	932,543	979,170	1,028,128	1,079,535	1,133,511	1,190,187	1,249,696	1,312,181	1,377,790	1,446,680	1,519,014
TOTAL SECTION 8/CHAPTER 707 INCOME	0	0	0	0	0	0	0	0	0	0	0	0	0	0	0	0
TOTAL TAX SYNDICATION	167,475	167,475	167,475	167,475	167,475	167,475	167,475	167,475	167,475	167,475	0	0	0	0	0	0
TOTAL SHARP INCOME	0	0	0	0	0	0	0	0	0	0	0	0	0	0	0	0
TOTAL INCOME AND SUBSIDIES:	898,146	934,680	973,040	1,013,318	1,055,611	1,100,017	1,146,645	1,195,603	1,247,010	1,300,986	1,190,187	1,249,696	1,312,181	1,377,790	1,446,680	1,519,014
EXPENSES																
OPERATING EXPENSES @ 63.50% NOF	(296,363)	(313,281)	(328,945)	(345,392)	(362,662)	(380,795)	(399,835)	(419,826)	(440,818)	(462,859)	(485,001)	(510,302)	(535,817)	(562,607)	(590,738)	(620,275)
REAL ESTATE TAXES @ 10.35% /SF	(60,984)	(65,033)	(69,285)	(93,349)	(96,437)	(100,259)	(104,527)	(113,963)	(119,661)	(125,633)	(131,915)	(138,510)	(145,436)	(152,708)	(160,343)	(168,360)
TOTAL EXPENSES	(379,247)	(398,314)	(418,230)	(439,141)	(461,099)	(484,153)	(533,779)	(560,460)	(588,482)	(617,946)	(644,812)	(681,259)	(715,315)	(751,081)	(788,635)	
NET OPERATING INCOME:	518,799	536,366	554,810	574,177	594,512	615,864	638,283	661,824	686,541	712,495	572,271	609,384	530,929	652,475	695,599	730,379
ANNUAL DEBT SERVICE:	(1,197,355)	(1,197,355)	(1,197,355)	(1,197,355)	(1,197,355)	(1,197,355)	(1,197,355)	(1,197,355)	(1,197,355)	(1,197,355)	(1,197,355)	(1,197,355)	(1,197,355)	(1,197,355)	(1,197,355)	(1,197,355)
BEFORE TAX CASH FLOW	(678,556)	(660,990)	(642,545)	(623,178)	(602,843)	(581,491)	(559,072)	(535,531)	(510,814)	(484,861)	(625,084)	(596,471)	(566,427)	(534,880)	(501,756)	(466,976)
HUD EFFECTIVE INDEX/DEBT	1.04%	4.18%	4.12%	4.47%	4.63%	4.80%	4.97%	5.16%	5.35%	5.55%	4.46%	4.85%	4.90%	3.16%	5.42%	3.69%
ROE INDEX/EQUITY	-55.25%	-34.34%	-33.38%	-32.37%	-31.32%	-30.21%	-29.04%	-27.829	-26.54%	-25.13%	-32.41%	-30.93%	-29.13%	-27.79%	-26.07%	-24.18%
GAP TO ACHIEVE ROE OF 15.00%	967,296	949,730	931,286	911,919	891,584	870,232	824,222	799,555	774,601	743,601	913,825	885,212	855,167	823,621	790,497	755,717

PV OF 15 YR GAP SUM @ 6.90%	47,803,152	
NOMINAL VALUE OF GAP SUM OVER 15 YRS	$14,025,610	

PV OF 15 YR SUBSIDY	$4,142,933	90
PV OF 10 YR TAX SYND		90
PV OF 15 YR SHARP		
TOTAL OF PV'S ABOVE	$4,142,933	

DEBT SERVICE CALCULATION
PRINCIPAL	$10,902,902
INTEREST RATE	10.50% PER YEAR
TERM	30 YEARS
MONTHLY PAYMENT	$99,780
YEARLY PAYMENT	$1,197,355

RENTAL ANALYSIS   PHASE 1B   VACANT PARCELS 49-14
PARCEL DESCRIPTION R11-E, PE-7B, 29-A, R-12A, R-12B, 33B
PREPARED BY THE BOSTON REDEVELOPMENT AUTHORITY

OPTION 1B   1b

		MON/YR I=0	1
		SEC 8=0	0
		SUBGRANT=0	0
		P SLIP=0	
		VR/HUD=0	
		MHFA=0	
		111C=0	
		INT	8.5%
		MGD	13.00%
		LON	33.00%
		CISE RATE	6.50%
		INFLA FTR	5.00%

DEVELOPMENT PROGRAM

PARCEL AREA	56,237 GSF
NUMBER OF UNITS	100 UNITS
PARKING SPACES	70 SPACES
EQUITY REQUIREMENT	15.00% OF TDL EQUITY

UNIT MIX:

		(NO INCOME LIMIT)				
MARKET RATE	33.0%	UNIT MORE THAN 80% OF BRSA MEDIAN INCOME				
MODERATE INCOME	33.0%	UNIT MORE THAN 50% OF BRSA MEDIAN INCOME				
LOW INCOME	33.0%					

UNIT COMPOSITION

	NO UNITS	% AGE	GSF	NSF	EFFICIENCY
MARKET RATE UNITS					
1 BEDROOM UNITS	17	50%	700	595	85.0%
2 BEDROOM UNITS	16	50%	900	765	85.0%
TOTAL MARKET RATE UNITS	33	100%	27,900	23,715	85.0%
MODERATE INCOME					
2 BEDROOM UNITS	22	67%	1,000	850	85.0%
3 BEDROOM UNITS	11	33%	1,245	1,058	85.0%
TOTAL MODERATE RATE UNITS	33	100%	35,695	30,341	85.0%
LOW INCOME					
2 BEDROOM UNITS	23	67%	1,000	850	85.0%
3 BEDROOM UNITS	11	33%	1,245	1,058	85.0%
TOTAL LOW INCOME UNITS	34	100%	36,695	31,191	85.0%
TOTAL	100		100,290	85,247	

DEVELOPMENT PRO FORMA:

	UNIT COST		TOTAL COST
LAND COST			
MARKET RATE UNITS	$25,000.00 /BU (FMV)		$825,000
MODERATE INCOME UNITS	$10,000.00 /BU (FMV)		$330,000
LOW INCOME UNITS	$5,000.00 /BU (FMV)		$170,000
TOTAL LAND COST			$1,325,000

HARD COSTS

RESIDENTIAL CONSTRUCTION PER GSF	$90		$9,026,100
TOTAL HARD AND LAND COSTS			$10,351,100

PROJECT RELATED SOFT COSTS

A/E FEE	6.0% OF HC	$541,566
LEGAL FEES	3.0% OF HC	$270,783
ACCOUNTING FEES	0.0% OF HC	$36,104
DEVELOPER'S FEE	4.0% OF HC	$361,044
RE TAXES DURING CONSTRUCTION		$69,663
INSURANCE, TITLE, PERMITS	1.0% OF HC	$90,261
RENT-UP AND MARKETING/MARKET	$4600 /UNIT	$119,800
RENT-UP AND MARKETING/LOW AND MOD	$3300 /UNIT	$820,000
RENT-UP DEFICIT	10.0%	$104,428
CONSTRUCTION INTEREST @	10.0%	$504,766
TOTAL SOFT COSTS		$2,630,516
TOTAL PROJECT COSTS		$12,304,616
CONTINGENCY (% OF HARD COSTS)	5.0%	$451,305
TOTAL DEVELOPMENT COST		$12,832,921
EQUITY REQUIREMENT	15.0%	$1,924,938
TDC/GSF		$127.96
TDC/1 BEDROOM UNIT		$89,571
TDC/2 BEDROOM UNIT		$127,958
TDC/3 BEDROOM UNIT		$159,380

RENTAL INCOME SCHEDULE (YEAR 1, FIRST STABILIZED YEAR)

	Monthly Income/Unit	Yearly Income
TENANT INCOME		
Market Rate Units:		
1 Bedroom	$750	$165,350
2 Bedroom	$1,000	$182,600
Moderate Income Units:		
2 Bedroom	$635	$159,258
3 Bedroom	$685	$465,899
Low Income Units:		
2 Bedroom	$897	$104,051
3 Bedroom	$1428	$53,671
TOTAL TENANT INCOME		$736,672

SECTION 8/CHAPTER 707 SUBSIDY INCOME		
Low Income:		
2 Bedroom	$273	$71,501
3 Bedroom	$412	$51,463
TOTAL SECTION 8/707 INCOME		$123,245

SYNDICATION - TAX CREDIT (10 YEARS)		
Low Income:		
2 Bedroom	$181	$49,470
3 Bedroom	$185	$24,963
TOTAL Syndication		$74,433

SHARP PROGRAM:		
Moderate Income:		
2 Bedroom	$270	$71,280
3 Bedroom	$325	$142,900
Low Income		
2 Bedroom	$270	$74,520
3 Bedroom	$325	$142,900
TOTAL SHARP INCOME		$231,600

GAP ANALYSIS (YEAR 1)

ASSUMPTIONS

OPTION	
MARKET=0	1
SEC 8=0	0
SHARP=0	0
SSR(MOD)=0	1
P-SHIP=0	0
VA IND=0	0
MFR=0	0
Irate	8.5%
INFLATION FACTOR	3.0%

OPERATING EXPENSES	($379,347)
DEBT SERVICE	($1,006,475)
TENANT INCOME	$736,672
GAP W/O SUBSIDY	($653,151)

GAP FROM ABOVE	($653,151)
SECTION 8 / CHAPTER 707 INCOME	$123,245
GAP	($531,905)

GAP FROM ABOVE	($531,905)
TAX CREDIT INCOME	$74,433
GAP	($457,472)

EXISTING GAP FROM ABOVE	($457,472)
SHARP INCOME	$231,600
FINAL BEFORE TAX CASH FLOW	($225,872)
GAP REQUIRED TO BREAK EVEN	($225,872)
GAP INCLUDING A RETURN ON EQUITY OF 6.6%	$352,918

OPERATING PRO FORMA (YEAR 1, FIRST STABILIZED YEAR)

TOTAL INCOME AND SUBSIDIES

Market Rate Units			
1 Bedroom	17	$750	$145,350
2 Bedroom	16	$1,000	$182,600
Moderate Income Units			
2 Bedroom	22	$633	$620,538
3 Bedroom	11	$976	$128,799
Low Income Units			
2 Bedroom	23	$1,087	$200,064
3 Bedroom	11	$1,309	$172,799
TOTAL INCOME AND SUBSIDIES			$1,159,950

(See income schedule for specific subsidy breakdowns)

EXPENSES:

Operating Expenses	$3.50/NSF	($298,363)
Real Estate Taxes	$0.95/NSF	($80,984)
TOTAL EXPENSES:		($379,347)
NET OPERATING INCOME:		$780,603
ANNUAL DEBT SERVICE:		
Principal	$10,907,982	
Interest Rate	10.50%	
Term (Years)	30	($1,006,475)
BEFORE TAX CASH FLOW (GAP)		($225,872)

FIFTEEN YEAR OPERATING PRO FORMA

CALENDAR YEAR
PROJECT YEAR
INFLATION/YEAR   5.0%

	1989	1990	1991	1992	1993	1994	1995	1996	1997	1998	1999	2000	2001	2002	2003	2004
	1	2	3	4	5	6	7	8	9	10	11	12	13	14	15	16

INCOME AND SUBSIDIES

	1	2	3	4	5	6	7	8	9	10	11	12	13	14	15	16
TOTAL TENANT INCOME	730,632	767,265	805,565	845,844	888,136	932,543	979,170	1,028,128	1,079,535	1,133,511	1,190,187	1,249,696	1,312,181	1,377,790	1,446,680	1,519,014
TOTAL SECTION 8/VOUCHER 707 INCOME	123,245	129,408	135,878	142,672	149,806	157,296	165,161	173,419	182,090	191,194	200,754	210,791	221,331	232,398	244,017	256,218
TOTAL TAX SYNDICATION	74,433	74,433	74,433	74,433	74,433	74,433	74,433	74,433	74,433	74,433						
TOTAL SHARP INCOME	231,600	220,620	209,019	198,568	188,640	179,208	170,247	161,725	153,648	145,966	138,667	131,734	32,214	64,550	45,185	0
TOTAL INCOME AND SUBSIDIES	1,159,950	1,191,466	1,224,896	1,261,517	1,301,014	1,343,479	1,389,011	1,437,715	1,489,706	1,545,105	1,529,608	1,592,222	1,625,726	1,674,738	1,735,882	1,775,232

EXPENSES

	13.50 /NSF	1	2	3	4	5	6	7	8	9	10	11	12	13	14	15	16
OPERATING EXPENSES		298,363	313,281	328,945	345,392	362,662	380,795	399,835	419,826	440,818	462,859	486,001	510,302	535,817	562,607	590,738	620,259
REAL ESTATE TAXES	40.95 /NSF	180,984	185,033	189,285	193,749	198,437	103,358	108,527	113,958	119,651	125,633	131,915	138,510	145,436	152,708	160,343	168,360
TOTAL EXPENSES		379,347	398,314	418,230	439,141	461,099	484,153	508,361	533,779	560,468	588,492	617,916	648,812	681,253	715,315	751,081	788,620
NET OPERATING INCOME		780,603	792,752	806,666	822,375	839,916	859,326	880,650	904,936	929,238	956,613	911,692	943,410	944,424	959,422	984,801	986,597
ANNUAL DEBT SERVICE		1,006,475	1,006,475	1,006,475	1,006,475	1,006,475	1,006,475	1,006,475	1,006,475	1,006,475	1,006,475	1,006,475	1,006,475	1,006,475	1,006,475	1,006,475	1,006,475
BEFORE TAX CASH FLOW		(225,872)	(213,724)	(199,810)	(184,100)	(166,560)	(147,149)	(125,826)	(102,539)	(77,238)	(49,862)	(94,783)	163,063	162,002	147,033	(21,674)	(19,879)
ROI (DEBT/EQUITY)		6.004	6.184	6.294	6.414	6.554	6.704	6.864	7.044	7.244	7.454	7.694	7.954	8.244	8.544	8.884	9.234
		-11.734	-11.109	-10.388	-9.565	-8.659	-7.644	-6.544	-5.339	-4.011	-2.594	-1.925	-3.289	-3.209	-2.445	-1.135	1.033
GAP TO ACHIEVE ROI OF	6.00%	152,918	140,769	126,856	111,146	93,606	74,195	52,871	29,585	204,284	176,908	821,829	190,311	185,044	174,099	148,720	146,924

								PV OF 15 YR BTCF/707 @	$1,479,720	6.90%
								PV OF 10 YR TAX SYND @	$567,980	6.90%
								PV OF 15 YR SHARP @	$1,503,694	6.90%
								TOTAL OF PV'S ABOVE	$3,491,393	

PV OF 15 YR GAP STRM @	6.90%	$2,339,147		
NOMINAL VALUE OF GAP STREAM 15 YRS		$3,646,946		

DEBT SERVICE CALCULATION:
PRINCIPAL	$10,907,982	PER YEAR
INTEREST RATE	8.50%	YEARS
TERM	30	
MONTHLY PAYMENT	$83,873	
YEARLY PAYMENT	$1,006,475	

RENTAL ANALYSIS PHASE 1B VACANT PARCELS V3 14
PARCEL DESCRIPTION: R11 C, RC 7A, 29-A, R 12A, R 12A, 13B
PREPARED BY THE BOSTON REDEVELOPMENT AUTHORITY

DEVELOPMENT PROGRAM

PARCEL AREA   54,237 GSF
NUMBER OF UNITS   100 UNITS
PARKING SPACES   70 SPACES

EQUITY REQUIREMENT   15 00% OF TDC EQUITY

UNIT MIX

MARKET RATE	33 0%
MODERATE INCOME	33 0%
LOW INCOME	33 0%

UNIT COMPOSITION:	NO. UNITS	% AGE	GSF	NSF	EFFICIENCY
		(NO INCOME LIMIT)			
MARKET RATE UNITS					
1 BEDROOM UNITS	17	50%	700	595	85 0%
2 BEDROOM UNITS	16	50%	1,000	850	85.0%
TOTAL MARKET RATE UNITS	33	100%	27,900	23,715	85.0%
		(NO MORE THAN 80% OF SMSA MEDIAN INCOME)			
MODERATE INCOME					
2 BEDROOM UNITS	22	67%	1,000	850	85.0%
3 BEDROOM UNITS	11	33%	1,245	1,058	85.0%
TOTAL MODERATE RATE UNITS	33	100%	25,695	30,341	85.0%
		(NO MORE THAN 50% OF SMSA MEDIAN INCOME)			
LOW INCOME					
2 BEDROOM UNITS	23	67%	1,000	850	85.0%
3 BEDROOM UNITS	11	33%	1,245	1,058	85.0%
TOTAL LOW INCOME UNITS	34	100%	36,695	31,191	85.0%
TOTAL	100		100,290	85,247	

DEVELOPMENT PRO FORMA

LAND COST

	UNIT COST	TOTAL COST
MARKET RATE UNITS	$25,000.00 /BU (FMV)	$825,000
MODERATE INCOME UNITS	$0.00 /BU (FMV)	$0
LOW INCOME UNITS	$0.00 /BU (FMV)	$0

TOTAL LAND COST $825,000

HARD COSTS
RESIDENTIAL CONSTRUCTION PER GSF $90 $9,026,100

TOTAL HARD AND LAND COSTS - $9,851,100

PROJECT RELATED SOFT COSTS
A&E FEE	6.0% OF HC	$541,326
LEGAL FEES	3.0% OF HC	$270,783
ACCOUNTING FEES	.0% OF HC	$36,104
DEVELOPER'S FEE	4.0% OF HC	$361,044
RE TAXES DURING CONSTRUCTION		$166,298
INSURANCE, TITLE, PERMITS		$90,261
RENT-UP 2ND MARKETING/MARKET	$600 /UNIT	$19,800
RENT-UP 2ND MARKETING/LOW MOD	$300 /UNIT	$20,100
RENT-UP DEFICIT	10.0%	$111,443

CONSTRUCTION INTEREST @   10.0% $483,164

TOTAL SOFT COSTS $2,000,522

TOTAL PROJECT COSTS $11,851,682

CONTINGENCY 15 OF HARD COSTS   5 0% $451,305

TOTAL DEVELOPMENT COST   15 0% $12,303,957
EQUITY REQUIREMENT $1,845,443

TDC/GSF $122 67

TDC/1 BEDROOM UNIT	$65,822
TDC/2 BEDROOM UNIT	$122,674
TDC/3 BEDROOM UNIT	$159 724

OPTION 1C
MON/PD I=0   0
SEC 8=0   0
SUBS/UN(+)=0   0
P=OUT(+)=0   0
KO/AND=0   0
LT(+)=0   1
INT RATE   8.5%
NET   0
MOD   33 00%
LOW   33 00%
DISC RATE   4 00%
INFLA FTR   3.00%

RENTAL INCOME SCHEDULE (YEAR 1, FIRST STABILIZED YEAR)

TENANT INCOME:	Monthly Income/Unit	Yearly Income
Market Rate Units:		
1 Bedroom	$750	$115,350
2 Bedroom	$1,000	$182,400
Moderate Income Un.ts:		
2 Bedroom	$635	$159,258
3 Bedroom	$685	$185,699
Low Income Units:		
2 Bedroom	$397	$104,493
3 Bedroom	$428	$133,671
TOTAL TENANT INCOME:		$430,672

SECTION 8/CHAPTER 707 SUBSIDY INCOME

	Monthly Income/Unit	Yearly Income
Low Income:		
2 Bedroom	$273	$71,581
3 Bedroom	$412	$51,663
TOTAL SECTION 8/707 INCOME:		$123,245

SYNDICATION - TAX CREDIT (10 YEARS)

	Monthly Income/Unit	Yearly Income
Low Income:		
2 Bedroom	$180	$49,740 :
3 Bedroom	$186	$124,499 :
TOTAL Syndication:		$74,239

SHARED PRINCIPAL

	Monthly Income/Unit	Yearly Income
Moderate Income:		
2 Bedroom	$270	$71,280
3 Bedroom	$325	$142,900
Low Income:		
2 Bedroom	$270	$74,520
3 Bedroom	$325	$142,900
TOTAL SHARED INCOME:		$231,600

GAP ANALYSIS (YEAR 1)

ASSUMPTIONS:

OPTION	
MARKET=0	0
SET 8=0	0
SHARED=0	0
SUBSIDY=0	1
D-SUBSIDY=0	1
BALANCE=0	1
MOD=0	1
Irate	8.5%
INFLATION FACTOR	5.0%

OPERATING EXPENSES	$379,347
DEBT SERVICE	$954,912
TENANT INCOME	$430,672
GAP W/O SUBSIDY	$613,587

GAP FROM ABOVE	$613,587

SECTION 8 / CHAPTER 707 INCOME	$123,245
GAP	$490,342

GAP FROM ABOVE	$490,342
TAX CREDIT INCOME	$74,239
GAP	$416,102

EXISTING GAP FROM ABOVE	$416,102
SHARED INCOME	$231,600
FINAL BEFORE TAX CASH FLOW	$184,502
GAP REQUIRED TO BREAK EVEN	$184,502
GAP INCLUDING A RETURN ON EQUITY OF 6.66%	$306,301

OPERATING AND FUNDING (YEAR 1, FIRST STABILIZED YEAR)

TOTAL INCOME AND SUBSIDIES:

Market Rate Units:		
1 Bedroom	17	$750	$115,350
2 Bedroom	16	$1,000	$182,400
Moderate Income Un.ts:		
2 Bedroom	22	$672	$220,538
3 Bedroom	11	$976	$128,799
Low Income Units:		
2 Bedroom	23	$1,087	$279,934
3 Bedroom	11	$1,399	$412,735

TOTAL INCOME AND SUBSIDIES	$1,339,756

(See income schedule for specific subsidy breakdowns)

EXPENSES:

Operating Expenses	$3.50 /NSF	$298,938
Real Estate Taxes	$0.95 /NSF	$800,984
TOTAL EXPENSES:		$379,347

NET OPERATING INCOME:	$980,410

ANNUAL DEBT SERVICE:		
Principal	$14,457,922	$954,912
Interest Rate	8.50%	
Term (Years)	30	

BEFORE TAX CASH FLOW (GAP)	$184,502

FIFTEEN YEAR OPERATING PRO FORMA

CALENDAR YEAR
PROJECT YEAR
INFLATION/YEAR   5.00%

INCOME AND SUBSIDIES

TOTAL TENANT INCOME:

TOTAL SECTION 8/COMPUTER 707 INCOME:

TOTAL TAX SYNDICATION:

TOTAL SHOP INCOME

TOTAL INCOME AND SUBSIDIES

EXPENSES:

OPERATING EXPENSES
REAL ESTATE TAXES

TOTAL EXPENSES

NET OPERATING INCOME

ANNUAL DEBT SERVICE:

BEFORE TAX CASH FLOW:

BOOK INDV/DEC
ROE (BEST/EQUITY)

GAP TO ACHIEVE ROE OF   6.00%

PV OF 15 YR GAP STREAM @   6.90%

NONBANK VALUE @ GAP STREAM 15 YRS

REAL SERVICE CALCULATION:
PRINCIPAL $10,457,522
INTEREST RATE   8.50% PER YEAR
YEAR   30 YEARS
MONTHLY PAYMENT $80,409
YEARLY PAYMENT $964,912

RENTAL ANALYSIS   PAGE 1B   VACANT PARCELS #1 - 14
PARCEL DESCRIPTION 114-C, RE-78, 29 A, 1-12A, A-12A, 11B
PREPARED BY THE BOSTON REDEVELOPMENT AUTHORITY

DEVELOPMENT PROGRAM

PARCEL AREA:	56,237 GSF
NUMBER OF UNITS:	100 UNITS
PARKING SPACES:	70 SPACES

EQUITY REQUIREMENT   15.00% OF TDC EQUITY

UNIT MIX

		IND INCOME LIMIT			
MARKET RATE INCOME	65.0%	NO LIMIT	80% OF SMSA MEDIAN INCOME		
MODERATE INCOME	17.5%	MORE THAN 80% OF SMSA MEDIAN INCOME			
LOW INCOME	17.5%	NOT MORE THAN 50% OF SMSA MEDIAN INCOME			

UNIT COMPOSITION	NO UNITS	% AGE	GSF	NSF	EFFICIENCY
MARKET RATE UNITS					
2 BEDROOM UNITS	32	50%	700	595	85.0%
3 BEDROOM UNITS	32	50%	1,000		85.0%
TOTAL MARKET RATE UNITS	64	100%	54,400	46,240	85.0%
MODERATE INCOME					
2 BEDROOM UNITS	12	67%	1,000	850	85.0%
3 BEDROOM UNITS	6	33%	1,245	1,058	85.0%
TOTAL MODERATE RATE UNITS	18	100%	19,410	16,500	85.0%
LOW INCOME					
2 BEDROOM UNITS	12	67%	1,000	850	85.0%
3 BEDROOM UNITS	6	33%	1,245	1,058	85.0%
TOTAL LOW INCOME UNITS	18	100%	19,410	16,500	85.0%
TOTAL	**100**		**93,340**	**79,339**	

DEVELOPMENT PRO FORMA

	UNIT COST	TOTAL COST
LAND COST		$1,600,000
MARKET RATE UNITS	$25,000.00 /DU (FMV)	
MODERATE INCOME UNITS	$0.00 /DU (FMV)	$0
LOW INCOME UNITS	$0.00 /DU (FMV)	$0
TOTAL LAND COST		$1,600,000

HARD COSTS		
RESIDENTIAL CONSTRUCTION PER GSF	$90	$8,400,600
TOTAL HARD AND LAND COSTS		$10,000,600

PROJECT RELATED SOFT COSTS		
A/E FEE	6.0% OF HC	$504,036
LEGAL FEES	3.0% OF HC	$252,018
ACCOUNTING FEES	0.4% OF HC	$33,602
DEVELOPER'S FEE	4.0% OF HC	$336,024
RE TAXES DURING CONSTRUCTION		$462,264
INSURANCE, TITLE, PERMITS	1.0% OF HC	$484,006
START-UP AND MARKETING/MARKET	$600 /UNIT	$38,400
START-UP AND MARKETING/LOW-MOD	$500 /UNIT	$18,000
RENT-UP DEFICIT	10.0%	$427,474

CONSTRUCTION INTEREST @	10 0%	$449,631

TOTAL SOFT COSTS		$2,834,296

CONTINGENCY (% OF HARD COSTS)	5.0%	$420,030

TOTAL DEVELOPMENT COST		$12,454,926
EQUITY REQUIREMENT	15.0%	$1,868,239

TDC/GSF		$133.44
TDC/1 BEDROOM UNIT		$93,405
TDC/2 BEDROOM UNIT		$112,436
TDC/3 BEDROOM UNIT		$155,729

RENTAL INCOME SCHEDULE YEAR 1, FIRST STABILIZED YEAR

	Monthly Income/Unit	Yearly Income
TENANT INCOME:		
Market Rate Units		
1 Bedroom	$750	$273,600
2 Bedroom	$1,000	$384,000
Moderate Income Units:		
2 Bedroom	$633	$106,068
3 Bedroom	$685	$145,634
Low Income Units:		
2 Bedroom	$397	$54,319
3 Bedroom	$420	$23,725
TOTAL TENANT INCOME		$453,707
SECTION 8/CHAPTER 707 SUBSIDY INCOME		
Low Income:		
2 Bedroom	$273	$37,346
3 Bedroom	$412	$23,181
TOTAL SECTION 8/707 INCOME		$65,527
SYNDICATION – TAX CREDIT (10 YEARS):		
Low Income		
2 Bedroom	$0	$0
3 Bedroom	$0	$0
TOTAL Syndication:		$0
SHARP PROGRAM:		
Moderate Income		
2 Bedroom	$270	$38,880
3 Bedroom	$325	$23,400
Low Income		
2 Bedroom	$270	$38,880
3 Bedroom	$325	$23,400
TOTAL SHARP INCOME:		$124,560

GAP ANALYSIS (YEAR 1)

ASSUMPTIONS

OPTION	
NEWOPT 1=0	1
SEC 8=1	0
SHARP=0	0
SUBLONG=0	0
P-SHRP=0	0
GLAND=0	0
MTFR=0	0
Irate	8.3%
INFLATION FACTOR	5.0%
OPERATING EXPENSES	(621,659)
DEBT SERVICE	(976,830)
TENANT INCOME	453,707
GAP W/O SUBSIDY	(474,181)

GAP FROM ABOVE	(474,181)
SECTION 8 / CHAPTER 707 INCOME	65,527
GAP	(408,654)

GAP FROM ABOVE	(408,654)
TAX CREDIT INCOME	0
GAP	(408,654)

EXISTING GAP FROM ABOVE	(408,654)
SHARP INCOME	124,560
FINAL BEFORE TAX CASH FLOW	(284,094)
GAP REQUIRED TO BREAK EVEN	(284,094)
GAP INCLUDING A RETURN ON EQUITY OF 6.05%	(440,398)

OPERATING FOR FROM (YEAR 1, FIRST STABILIZED YEAR)

TOTAL INCOME AND SUBSIDIES

Market Rate Units		
1 Bedroom	32	$273,600
2 Bedroom	32	$384,000
Moderate Income Units:		
2 Bedroom	12	$125,748
3 Bedroom	6	$145,254
Low Income Units:		
2 Bedroom	12	$130,336
3 Bedroom	6	$160,856
TOTAL INCOME AND SUBSIDIES		$1,045,794
(See income schedule for specific subsidy breakdown)		

EXPENSES:

Operating Expenses	$3.50 /NSF	$227,687
Real Estate Taxes	$0.35 /NSF	$145,322
TOTAL EXPENSES:		$353,059
NET OPERATING INCOME:		$432,725
ANNUAL DEBT SERVICE:		$976,830
Principal $13,506,147		
Interest Rate 8.3%		
Term (Years) 30		
BEFORE TAX CASH FLOW (BTCF)		(824,094)

-71-

FIFTEEN YEAR OPERATING PRO FORMA

CN ANNUM YEAR
PROJECT YEAR
INFLATION/YEAR   5.00%

INCOME AND SUBSIDIES

TOTAL TENANT INCOME:

TOTAL SECTION 8/CHAPTER 707 INCOME:

TOTAL TAX SUBSIDIZATION:

TOTAL SUBSIDY INCOME

TOTAL INCOME AND SUBSIDIES

EXPENSES

OPERATING EXPENSES
REAL ESTATE TAXES

TOTAL EXPENSES

NET OPERATING INCOME:

ANNUAL DEBT SERVICE

BEFORE TAX CASH FLOW

RDHFC PROV(INC)
PER UNIT/FACILITY

GAP TO ACHIEVE ROE OF

PV OF 15 YR GAP STREAM @

NOMINAL VALUE OF GAP STREAM 15 YRS

DEBT SERVICE CALCULATION:
PRINCIPAL
INTEREST RATE
TERM
MONTHLY PAYMENT
YEARLY PAYMENT

-72-

RENTAL ANALYSIS   PAGE 18   VACANT PARCELS #3 - 14
PARCEL DESCRIPTION H3-4, H5-6, C2-4, R 12A, R 12B, 33B
PREPARED BY THE BOSTON REDEVELOPMENT AUTHORITY

DEVELOPMENT PROGRAM

PARCEL AREA   50,237 GSF
NUMBER OF UNITS   100 UNITS
PARKING SPACES   70 SPACES

EQUITY REQUIREMENT   15.00% OF DC EQUITY

UNIT MIX

		(NO INCOME LIMIT)					
MARKET RATE	50.0%	(NO INCOME LIMIT)					
MODERATE INCOME	25.0%	(NOT MORE THAN 80% OF SMSA MEDIAN INCOME)					
LOW INCOME	25.0%	(NOT MORE THAN 50% OF SMSA MEDIAN INCOME)					

UNIT COMPOSITION	NO. UNITS	% AGE	GSF	NSF	EFFICIENCY
MARKET RATE UNITS					
2 BEDROOM UNITS	25	50%	700	595	85.0%
3 BEDROOM UNITS	25	50%	1,000	850	85.0%
TOTAL MARKET RATE UNITS	50	100%	42,500	36,125	85.0%
MODERATE INCOME					
2 BEDROOM UNITS	17	67%	1,000	850	85.0%
3 BEDROOM UNITS	8	33%	1,295	1,058	85.0%
TOTAL MODERATE RATE UNITS	25	100%	26,960	22,916	85.0%
LOW INCOME					
2 BEDROOM UNITS	17	67%	1,000	850	85.0%
3 BEDROOM UNITS	8	33%	1,295	1,058	85.0%
TOTAL LOW INCOME UNITS	25	100%	26,960	22,916	85.0%
TOTAL	100		96,420	81,957	

DEVELOPMENT PRO FORMA:

LAND COST	UNIT COST	TOTAL COST
		$1,250,000
MARKET RATE UNITS	$25,000.00 /BU (FMV)	$0
MODERATE INCOME UNITS	$0.00 /BU (FMV)	$0
LOW INCOME RATES	$0.00 /BU (FMV)	$0
TOTAL LAND COST:		$1,250,000

HARD COSTS

| RESIDENTIAL CONSTRUCTION PER GSF | $90 | $8,677,800 |

| TOTAL HARD AND LAND COSTS | | $9,927,800 |

PROJECT RELATED SOFT COSTS
A/E FEE	6.0% OF HC	$520,668
LEGAL FEES	3.0% OF HC	$260,334
ACCOUNTING FEES	0.44% OF HC	$43,711
DEVELOPER'S FEE	4.0% OF HC	$347,112
RE TAXES DURING CONSTRUCTION		$465,814
INSURANCE, TITLE, PERMITS	1.0% OF HC	$86,778
RENT-UP AND MARKETING/MARKET	$600 /UNIT	$30,000
RENT-UP AND MARKETING/LOW-MOD	$260 /UNIT	$13,000
RENT-UP DEFICIT	10.0%	$163,338

| CONSTRUCTION INTEREST @ | 10.0% | $486,989 |

| TOTAL SOFT COSTS | | $2,017,744 |

| TOTAL PROJECT COSTS | | $11,945,544 |

| CONTINGENCY 1% OF HARD COSTS | 5.0% | $433,890 |

| TOTAL DEVELOPMENT COST | | $12,379,434 |
| EQUITY REQUIREMENT | 15.0% | $1,856,915 |

| TDC/GSF | | $128.39 |

TDC/1 BEDROOM UNIT		$109,874
TDC/2 BEDROOM UNIT		$126,311
TDC/3 BEDROOM UNIT		$157,446

OPTION IE   Ie

NUMPROJ=0   1
SEC 8=0   0
SHRP=0   0
SERLAND=0   0
P-SHIP=0   0
ALL RES=0   0
W/F=0   0
LIHTC=1   1
MKT   8.5%
LOW   50.00%
DISC RATE   25.00%
INFLA FTR   6.50%
                 5.00%

-73-

1(e)

RENTAL INCOME SCHEDULE (YEAR 1, FIRST STABILIZED YEAR)

	Monthly Income/Unit	Yearly Income
TENANT INCOME		
Market Rate Units		
1 Bedroom	$750	$213,750
2 Bedroom	$1,000	$285,000
Moderate Income Units		
2 Bedroom	$635	$123,063
3 Bedroom	$685	$62,472
Low Income Units		
2 Bedroom	$397	$76,939
3 Bedroom	$428	$39,024
TOTAL TENANT INCOME:		$800,257

SECTION 8/CHAPTER 707 SUBSIDY INCOME

Low Income		
2 Bedroom	$273	$52,907
3 Bedroom	$412	$37,574
TOTAL SECTION 8/707 INCOME:		$90,482

SYNDICATION - TAX CREDIT (10 YEARS)

Low Income		
2 Bedroom	$179	$36,538
3 Bedroom	$187	$17,996
TOTAL Syndication:		$54,534

SHARP PROGRAM

Moderate Income		
2 Bedroom	$270	$55,600
3 Bedroom	$325	$31,200
Low Income		
2 Bedroom	$270	$53,060
3 Bedroom	$325	$31,200
TOTAL SHARP INCOME:		$172,560

GAP ANALYSIS (YEAR 1)

ASSUMPTIONS:

OPTION
MOD/MKT=0
SEC 8=0
SHRP=0
SUB/IND=0
P-SHIP=0
W/UND=0
MFR=0
Infl. Rate   8.5%
              5.0%

OPERATING EXPENSES	($634,709)
DEBT SERVICE	($970,909)
TENANT INCOME	$800,257
GAP W/O SUBSIDY	($535,360)
GAP FROM ABOVE	($535,360)
SECTION 8 / CHAPTER 707 INCOME	$90,482
GAP	($444,878)
GAP FROM ABOVE	($444,878)
TAX CREDIT INCOME	$54,534
GAP	($390,344)
EXISTING GAP FROM ABOVE	($390,344)
SHARP INCOME	$172,560
FINAL BEFORE TAX CASH FLOW	($217,784)
GAP REQUIRED TO BREAK EVEN	($217,784)
GAP INCLUDING A RETURN ON EQUITY OF 6.0%	$340,341

OPERATING PRO FORMA (YEAR 1, FIRST STABILIZED YEAR)

TOTAL INCOME AND SUBSIDIES:

Market Rate Units		
1 Bedroom	285	$750	$213,750
2 Bedroom	285	$1,000	$285,000
Moderate Income Units		
2 Bedroom	17	$873	$178,143
3 Bedroom	6	$996	$93,622
Low Income Units		
2 Bedroom	17	$1,066	$221,464
3 Bedroom	6	$1,310	$125,604
TOTAL INCOME AND SUBSIDIES			$1,117,633

(See income schedule for specific subsidy breakdowns)

EXPENSES:

Operating Expenses	$3.50 /NSF	$636,050
Real Estate Taxes	$0.95 /NSF	$177,659
TOTAL EXPENSES:		$834,709

NET OPERATING INCOME:	$353,125

ANNUAL DEBT SERVICE:
Principal $10,522,519
Interest Rate   9.50%
Term (Years)   30

$970,909

BEFORE TAX CASH FLOW (BTCF)	($217,784)

-74-

I(e)

FIFTEEN YEAR OPERATING PRO FORMA

CALENDAR YEAR	1989	1990	1991	1992	1993	1994	1995	1996	1997	1998	1999	2000	2001	2002	2003	2004
PROJECT YEAR	1	2	3	4	5	6	7	8	9	10	11	12	13	14	15	16
INFLATION/YEAR 5.00%																

INCOME AND SUBSIDIES

TOTAL TENANT INCOME	800,257	840,270	882,284	926,398	972,718	1,021,354	1,072,421	1,126,042	1,182,344	1,241,462	1,303,535	1,368,711	1,437,147	1,509,004	1,584,455	1,663,677
TOTAL SECTION 8/CHAPTER 707 INCOME	90,482	95,006	99,756	104,744	109,981	115,480	121,254	127,317	133,683	140,367	147,385	154,755	162,492	170,617	179,148	188,105
TOTAL TAX SYNDICATION	54,534	54,534	54,534	54,534	54,534	54,534	54,534	54,534	54,534	54,534	0	0	0	0	0	0
TOTAL SUBSIDY INCOME	172,560	163,932	155,735	147,949	140,551	133,524	126,847	120,505	114,480	108,756	103,318	98,152	63,707	48,495	33,666	0
TOTAL INCOME AND SUBSIDIES	1,117,833	1,153,742	1,192,309	1,233,625	1,277,784	1,324,892	1,375,057	1,428,399	1,485,041	1,545,119	1,554,238	1,621,618	1,660,346	1,727,716	1,797,268	1,851,782

EXPENSES

OPERATING EXPENSES 43.50 /NSF	(686,650)	(801,192)	(816,521)	(832,664)	(848,667)	(865,101)	(884,061)	(903,626)	(923,807)	(944,798)	(967,240)	(990,610)	(1,015,140)	(1,040,898)	(1,067,942)	(1,096,348)
REAL ESTATE TAXES 40.95 /NSF	(177,658)	(181,352)	(185,840)	(190,328)	(194,838)	(199,330)	(204,438)	(209,556)	(215,033)	(220,785)	(226,824)	(233,776)	(239,824)	(246,855)	(254,156)	(161,864)
TOTAL EXPENSES	(864,709)	(982,944)	(1,002,911)	(1,022,784)	(1,043,336)	(1,065,471)	(1,088,744)	(1,113,182)	(1,138,841)	(1,565,283)	(994,072)	(1,623,776)	(1,654,964)	(1,687,713)	(1,702,098)	(1,758,203)

NET OPERATING INCOME	753,125	770,798	789,218	811,429	834,479	859,421	866,313	903,217	946,200	979,336	960,166	997,843	1,011,384	1,040,003	1,085,170	1,053,579
ANNUAL DEBT SERVICE	(970,909)	(970,909)	(970,909)	(970,909)	(970,909)	(970,909)	(970,909)	(970,909)	(970,909)	(970,909)	(970,909)	(970,909)	(970,909)	(970,909)	(970,909)	(970,909)
BEFORE TAX CASH FLOW	(217,784)	(200,111)	(189,691)	(159,480)	(136,430)	(111,480)	(104,596)	(55,692)	(24,709)	8,427	118,743	26,934	42,473	53,094	104,261	122,671

BDTIC LIABILITIES	6.08%	6.23%	6.38%	6.55%	6.74%	6.94%	7.16%	7.39%	7.64%	7.91%	7.94%	8.06%	8.19%	8.46%	8.59%	8.83%
R.E. (BATT/EQUITY)	-11.73	-10.78	-9.73	-8.59	-7.35	-6.04	-5.64	-3.06	-1.33	0.45	-0.58	1.58	2.29	3.73	5.61	6.61

GRP TO ACHIEVE BDE DF 6.06%	8340,241	8322,667	8303,247	8282,635	8258,987	8234,045	8207,153	8178,248	8117,285	8114,189	8132,299	895,623	880,084	832,462	848,295	10

PV OF 15 YR GRP STRM @ 6.06%	81,085,332
NOMINAL VALUE OF GRP STREAM 15 YRS	82,764,000

PV OF 15 YR SUBSIDY @   84,086,258
PV OF 15 YR TAX SYND @   372,176
PV OF 15 YR SYND @   41,120,461

TOTAL OF PV'S ABOVE   82,578,895

DEBT SERVICE CALCULATION:
FINANCED $10,522,519
INTEREST RATE   8.25% PER YEAR
TERM   30 YEARS
MONTHLY PAYMENT $80,909
YEARLY PAYMENT $970,909

II(a)

AGENCY INCOME SCHEDULE (YEAR 1, FIRST STABILIZED YEAR)

	Monthly Income/Unit	Yearly Income
TENANT INCOME		
Market Rate Units		
1 Bedroom	$750	$145,350
2 Bedroom	$1,000	$182,400
Moderate Income Units		
2 Bedroom	$635	$159,258
3 Bedroom	$685	$185,899
Low Income Units		
2 Bedroom	$397	$104,093
3 Bedroom	$428	$153,671
TOTAL TENANT INCOME:		$730,622

SECTION 8/CHAPTER 707 SUBSIDY INCOME
Low Income:		
2 Bedroom	$0	$0
3 Bedroom	$0	$0
TOTAL SECTION 8/707 INCOME:		$0

SYNDICATION - TAX CREDIT (10 YEARS)
Low Income:		
2 Bedroom	$355	$109,061
3 Bedroom	$407	$53,717
TOTAL Syndication:		$162,778

SHARP PROGRAM
Moderate Income		
2 Bedroom	$0	$0
3 Bedroom	$0	$0
Low Income:		
2 Bedroom	$0	$0
3 Bedroom	$0	$0
TOTAL SHARP INCOME:		$0

GAP ANALYSIS (YEAR 1)

ASSUMPTIONS
INFLATION	
RENT (Y-0)	0
SEC 8-0	---
SHARP-0	---
SUBSIDY-0	---
P-SUB=0	---
RA INC-0	---
INFL-0	---
Trate	10.5%
INFLATION FACTOR	5.0%
OPERATING EXPENSES	($379,347)
DEBT SERVICE	($1,235,902)
TENANT INCOME	$730,622
GAP W/O SUBSIDY	($884,527)

GAP FROM ABOVE	($884,527)
SECTION 8 / CHAPTER 707 INCOME	$0
GAP	($884,527)

GAP FROM ABOVE	($884,527)
TAX CREDIT INCOME	$162,778
GAP	($721,800)

EXISTING GAP FROM ABOVE	($721,800)
SHARP INCOME	$0
FINAL BEFORE TAX CASH FLOW	($721,800)
GAP REQUIRED TO BREAK EVEN	($721,800)
GAP INCLUDING A RETURN ON EQUITY OF 15 DOS	$993,452

OPERATING PRO FORMA (YEAR 1, FIRST STABILIZED YEAR)

TOTAL INCOME AND SUBSIDIES
Market Rate Units:			
1 Bedroom	17	$750	$145,350
2 Bedroom	16	$1,000	$182,400
Moderate Income Units:			
2 Bedroom	22	$603	$159,258
3 Bedroom	11	$653	$185,899
Low Income Units:			
2 Bedroom	23	$377	$213,154
3 Bedroom	11	$814	$101,388
TOTAL INCOME AND SUBSIDIES			$893,449

(See income schedule for specific subsidy breakdowns)

EXPENSES:
Operating Expenses	$3.30 /NSF	($298,363)
Real Estate Taxes	$6.55 /NSF	($80,984)
TOTAL EXPENSES:		($379,347)
NET OPERATING INCOME:		$514,102
ANNUAL DEBT SERVICE:		($1,235,902)
Principal $11,255,147		
Interest Rate 14.26%		
Term (Years) 30		
BEFORE TAX CASH FLOW (GAP)		($721,800)

-77-

FIFTEEN YEAR OPERATING PRO FORMA

COLORADO YEAR	1989	1990	1991	1992	1993	1994	1995	1996	1997	1998	1999	2000	2001	2002	2003	2004
PROJECT YEAR	1	2	3	4	5	6	7	8	9	10	11	12	13	14	15	16
INFLATION/MERA 5 Out																
INCOME AND SUBSIDIES:																
TOTAL TENANT INCOME	730,672	767,205	805,565	845,844	888,136	932,543	979,170	1,028,128	1,079,535	1,133,511	1,190,187	1,249,696	1,312,181	1,377,790	1,446,680	1,519,014
TOTAL SECTION 8/CHAPTER 707 INCOME	0	0	0	0	0	0	0	0	0	0	0	0	0	0	0	0
TOTAL TAX SYNDICATION	162,778	162,778	162,778	162,778	162,778	162,778	162,778	162,778	162,778	162,778	0	0	0	0	0	0
TOTAL SHARP INCOME	0	0	0	0	0	0	0	0	0	0	0	0	0	0	0	0
TOTAL INCOME AND SUBSIDIES	893,449	929,983	968,343	1,008,621	1,050,914	1,095,320	1,141,948	1,190,906	1,242,312	1,296,289	1,190,187	1,249,696	1,312,181	1,377,790	1,446,680	1,519,014
EXPENSES:																
OPERATING EXPENSES @	(258,363)	(314,081)	(329,943)	(345,392)	(362,662)	(380,790)	(399,833)	(419,826)	(440,818)	(462,859)	(486,001)	(510,302)	(535,817)	(562,607)	(590,738)	(620,275)
REAL ESTATE TAXES @	(180,984)	(185,033)	(189,285)	(93,749)	(96,431)	(103,208)	(108,523)	(113,553)	(119,631)	(125,633)	(131,915)	(138,510)	(145,436)	(152,708)	(160,343)	(168,360)
TOTAL EXPENSES	(379,347)	(498,314)	(514,330)	(439,141)	(461,699)	(484,153)	(508,361)	(533,779)	(560,460)	(588,492)	(617,916)	(648,812)	(681,253)	(715,314)	(751,081)	(788,620)
NET OPERATING INCOME	514,102	531,669	556,113	569,480	589,815	611,167	633,586	657,127	581,844	707,798	572,271	600,884	630,909	662,425	695,599	730,379
ANNUAL DEBT SERVICE	11,235,900	11,235,900	11,235,900	11,235,900	11,235,900	11,235,900	11,235,900	11,235,900	11,235,900	11,235,900	11,235,900	11,235,900	11,235,900	11,235,900	11,235,900	11,235,900
BEFORE TAX CASH FLOW	1,721,000	1,704,243	1,683,789	1,666,420	1,646,087	1,624,735	1,602,316	1,578,775	1,554,058	1,528,100	1,663,631	1,635,018	1,604,993	1,573,477	1,540,303	1,505,523
DEPR. INDIRECT	4,118	4,258	4,404	4,558	4,718	4,894	5,065	5,253	5,464	5,665	5,874	6,095	5,045	5,388	3,364	3,841
RICE INFO/EQUITY	-57,786	-56,356	-54,824	-53,274	-51,644	-49,944	-48,135	-46,264	-44,254	-42,213	-53,055	-50,763	-48,358	-45,844	-43,176	-40,411
GAP TO ACHIEVE ROE @ 6.648	1804,367	1786,041	1768,155	1748,989	1728,654	9107,302	1684,883	1661,342	1636,625	1610,672	9746,798	9717,505	9687,541	9655,594	9622,870	9588,090
14 OF 15 YR GAP STRM @ 6.90%	16,309,200															
NOMINAL VALUE OF GAP STREAM 15 YRS	010,568,179															

PV OF 13 YR SH/CHP707 @   80
PV OF 80 YR TAX STRM @   80
PV OF 83 YR SHARP @   0

TOTAL OF PV'S ABOVE $4,110,899

$4,110,899

DEBT SERVICE CALCULATION:
PRINCIPAL $11,259,147
INTEREST RATE   10.50% PER YEAR
TERM   30 YEARS
MONTHLY PAYMENT $102,992
YEARLY PAYMENT $1,235,900

11b

RENTAL ANALYSIS   PHASE 1B VACANT PARCELS 49 - 14
PARCEL IDENTIFICATION #1 E, JR, JR, #, #, #, #, G-16M, 33B
PREPARED BY THE BOSTON REDEVELOPMENT AUTHORITY

DEVELOPMENT PROGRAM

PARCEL AREA   54,237 GSF
NUMBER OF UNITS   100 UNITS
PARKING SPACES   70 SPACES

EQUITY REQUIREMENT   10.00% OF TDC EQUITY

UNIT MIX:

		2ND INCOME LIMITS			
MARKET RATE	33.0%	UNIT MORE THAN 80% OF SMSA MEDIAN INCOME
MODERATE INCOME	33.0%	UNIT MORE THAN 80% OF SMSA MEDIAN INCOME
LOW INCOME	33.0%	UNIT MORE 50% OF SMSA MEDIAN INCOME

UNIT COMPOSITION:

	NO UNITS	% AGE	GSF	NSF	EFFICIENCY
MARKET RATE UNITS					
1 BEDROOM UNITS	17	50%	700	595	85.0%
2 BEDROOM UNITS	16	50%	1,000	850	85.0%
TOTAL MARKET RATE UNITS	33	100%	2,900	23,775	85.0%
MODERATE INCOME					
2 BEDROOM UNITS	22	67%	1,000	850	85.0%
3 BEDROOM UNITS	11	33%	1,245	1,058	85.0%
TOTAL MODERATE RATE UNITS	33	100%	25,655	36,341	85.0%
LOW INCOME					
2 BEDROOM UNITS	23	67%	1,000	850	85.0%
3 BEDROOM UNITS	11	33%	1,245	1,058	85.0%
TOTAL LOW INCOME UNITS	34	100%	36,425	31,141	85.0%
TOTAL	100		100,290	85,247	

DEVELOPMENT PRO FORMA

LAND COST

	UNIT COST	TOTAL COST
MARKET RATE UNITS	$25,000.00 /BU (FMR)	$825,000
MODERATE INCOME UNITS	$10,000.00 /BU (FMR)	$330,000
LOW INCOME UNITS	$3,000.00 /BU (FMR)	$170,000
TOTAL LAND COST:		$1,325,000

HARD COSTS
RESIDENTIAL CONSTRUCTION PER GSF $90 $9,626,100

TOTAL HARD AND LAND COSTS $10,351,100

PROJECT RELATED SOFT COSTS
A&E FEE	4.0% OF HC	$361,044
LEGAL FEES	1.5% OF HC	$135,392
ACCOUNTING FEES	0.25% OF HC	$18,052
DEVELOPER FEE	4.0% OF HC	$361,044
RE TAXES DURING CONSTRUCTION		$65,563
INSURANCE, TITLE, PERMITS		$96,261
RENT UP AND MARKETING/MARKET	1.0% OF HC	$119,261
RENT UP AND MARKETING/SUBSIDIZED	$300/UNIT	$30,100
RENT UP DEFICIT	10.0%	$813,122

CONSTRUCTION INTEREST @   10.0% $515,201

TOTAL SOFT COSTS $4,301,725

TOTAL PROJECT COSTS $12,650,859

CONTINGENCY (% OF HARD COSTS)   5.0% $451,305

TOTAL DEVELOPMENT COST $12,590,164
EQUITY REQUIREMENT   10.0% $1,251,016

TDC/GSF $129.71

TDC/1 BEDROOM UNIT $87,318
TDC/2 BEDROOM UNIT $105,140
TDC/3 BEDROOM UNIT $155,501

-79-

RENTAL INCOME SCHEDULE (YEAR 1, FIRST STABILIZED YEAR)

	Monthly Income/Unit	Yearly Income
TENANT INCOME:		
Market Rate Units:		
1 Bedroom	$750	$45,250
2 Bedroom	$1,000	$182,600
Moderate Income Units:		
2 Bedroom	$653	$159,250
3 Bedroom	$635	$63,999
Low Income Units:		
2 Bedroom	$397	$104,493
3 Bedroom	$438	$53,671
TOTAL TENANT INCOME:		$730,672

SECTION 8/CHAPTER 707 SUBSIDY INCOME

Low Income:		
2 Bedroom	$823	$71,581
3 Bedroom	$942	$53,663
TOTAL SECTION 8/707 INCOME:		$123,245

SYNDICATION - TAX CREDIT (10 YEARS):

Low Income:		
2 Bedroom	$176	$46,432
3 Bedroom	$188	$25,874
TOTAL Syndication:		$72,346

SHARP PROGRAM:

Moderate Income:		
2 Bedroom	$296	$71,289
3 Bedroom	$325	$42,500
Low Income:		
2 Bedroom	$290	$74,520
3 Bedroom	$325	$42,500
TOTAL SHARP INCOME		$231,600

GAP ANALYSIS (YEAR 1)

ASSUMPTIONS:

OPTION		
RENT-0		0
SEC 8-0		0
SHARP-0		0
SYN (AHP)-0		0
P SHIP-0		---
HIME-0		8.5%
Rate		5.0%
INFLATION FACTOR		
OPERATING EXPENSES		(477,247)
DEBT SERVICE		(1,038,877)
TENANT INCOME		$730,672
GAP W/O SUBSIDY		(467,553)

GAP FROM ABOVE		(467,553)
SECTION 8 / CHAPTER 707 INCOME		$123,245
GAP		(656,367)
GAP FROM ABOVE		(656,367)
TAX CREDIT INCOME		$72,346
GAP		(491,561)
EXISTING GAP FROM ABOVE		(491,561)
SHARP INCOME		$231,600
FINAL BEFORE TAX CASH FLOW		(656,361)
GAP REQUIRED TO BREAK EVEN		(656,361)
GAP INCLUDING A RETURN ON EQUITY OF: 6.00%		6,142,929

OPERATING PRO FORMA (YEAR 1, FIRST STABILIZED YEAR)

TOTAL INCOME AND SUBSIDIES:

Market Rate Units:			
1 Bedroom	17	$750	$165,250
2 Bedroom	15	$1,000	$182,600
Moderate Income Units:			
2 Bedroom	22	$653	$230,538
3 Bedroom	8	$635	$128,799
Low Income Units:			
2 Bedroom	23	$1,492	$298,666
3 Bedroom	11	$1,304	$172,110
TOTAL INCOME AND SUBSIDIES			$1,151,863

(See income schedule for specific subsidy breakdown)

EXPENSES:

Operating Expenses	$3.50/NSF	(429,513)
Real Estate Taxes	$0.95/NSF	(46,964)
TOTAL EXPENSES:		(477,247)
NET OPERATING INCOME:		$674,516
ANNUAL DEBT SERVICE:		(1,038,877)
Principal	$11,229,142	
Interest Rate	8.50%	
Term (Years)	30	
BEFORE TAX CASH FLOW (GAP)		(656,361)

IIb

RENTAL ANALYSIS PHASE 1B VACANT PARCELS #3-14
PARCEL DESCRIPTION: R11-5, R6-78, C2-A, F-128, R 12A, 13A
PREPARED BY THE BOSTON REDEVELOPMENT AUTHORITY

DEVELOPMENT PROGRAM

PARCEL AREA   50,223 GSF
NUMBER OF UNITS   100 UNITS
PARKING SPACES   70 SPACES

EQUITY REQUIREMENT   10.00% OF TDC EQUITY

UNIT MIX	MARKET RATE	MODERATE INCOME	LOW INCOME
	33.0%	33.0%	33.0%

UNIT COMPOSITION:	NO. UNITS	1 AGE	NO INCOME LIMIT	GSF	NSF	EFFICIENCY
MARKET RATE UNITS						
1 BEDROOM UNITS	17	50%		700	595	85.0%
2 BEDROOM UNITS	16	50%		1,000	850	85.0%
TOTAL MARKET RATE UNITS	33	100%		27,900	23,715	85.0%
MODERATE INCOME						
2 BEDROOM UNITS	22	67%		1,000	850	85.0%
3 BEDROOM UNITS	11	33%		1,215	1,058	85.0%
TOTAL MODERATE RATE UNITS	33	100%		25,685	24,341	85.0%
LOW INCOME						
2 BEDROOM UNITS	23	67%		1,000	850	85.0%
3 BEDROOM UNITS	11	33%		1,215	1,058	85.0%
TOTAL LOW INCOME UNITS	34	100%		36,695	31,191	85.0%
TOTAL	100			100,290	85,247	

DEVELOPMENT AND FUNDING

LAND COST	UNIT COST		TOTAL COST
			$825,000
MARKET RATE UNITS	$25,000.00 /DU (FMV)		$0
MODERATE INCOME UNITS	$0.00 /DU (FMV)		$0
LOW INCOME UNITS	$0.00 /DU (FMV)		$0

TOTAL LAND COST $825,000

HARD COSTS
RESIDENTIAL CONSTRUCTION PER GSF $90 $9,026,100

TOTAL HARD AND LAND COSTS $9,851,100

PROJECT RELATED SOFT COSTS
A/E FEE	1.0% OF HC	$131,044
LEGAL FEES	1.5% OF HC	$135,392
ACCOUNTING FEES	0.25% OF HC	$184,052
DEVELOPER'S FEE	4.0% OF HC	$361,044
RE TAXES DURING CONSTRUCTION		$44,828
INSURANCE, TITLE, PERMITS	1.0% OF HC	$90,261
RENT-UP AND MARKETING/MARKET	$600 /UNIT	$19,800
RENT-UP AND MARKETING/LOW MOD	$300 /UNIT	$20,100
RENT-UP DEFICIT	16.0%	$408,129

CONSTRUCTION INTEREST @   10.0% $1,676,535

TOTAL SOFT COSTS $1,676,535

TOTAL PROJECT COSTS $11,527,635

CONTINGENCY 1% OF HARD COSTS(1)   5.0% $501,305

TOTAL DEVELOPMENT COST $11,028,940
EQUITY REQUIREMENT   10.0% $11,187,894

TDC/GSF $119.44

TDC/1 BEDROOM UNIT	$83,639
TDC/2 BEDROOM UNIT	$119,443
TDC/3 BEDROOM UNIT	$146,707

-83-

IId

RENTAL INCOME SCHEDULE (YEAR 1, FIRST STABILIZED YEAR)

	Monthly Income/Unit	Yearly Income
TENANT INCOME		
Market Rate Units		
1 Bedroom	$750	$273,600
2 Bedroom	$1,000	$364,800
Moderate Income Units:		
2 Bedroom	$635	$86,868
3 Bedroom	$685	$46,854
Low Income Units		
2 Bedroom	$397	$54,310
3 Bedroom	$428	$29,275
TOTAL TENANT INCOME:		$855,707
SECTION 8/CHAPTER 707 SUBSIDY INCOME		
Low Income		
2 Bedroom	$273	$37,346
3 Bedroom	$412	$28,181
TOTAL SECTION 8/707 INCOME:)		$65,527
SYNDICATION TAX CREDIT (10 YEARS)		
Low Income		
2 Bedroom	$0	$0
3 Bedroom	$0	$0
TOTAL Syndication:)		$0
SHARP PROGRAM		
Moderate Income		
2 Bedroom	$270	$38,880
3 Bedroom	$325	$23,400
Low Income:		
2 Bedroom	$270	$38,880
3 Bedroom	$325	$23,400
TOTAL SHARP INCOME:)		$124,560

GAP ANALYSIS (YEAR 1)

ASSUMPTIONS	
OPTION	
NONPRFT=0	0
SEC 8=0	0
SHARP=0	0
SUBLAND=0	0
P SHIP=0	1
$0LAND=0	1
MHFA=0	0
Irate	8.5%
INFLATION FACTOR	5.0%
OPERATING EXPENSES	($353,059)
DEBT SERVICE	($1,009,196)
TENANT INCOME	$855,707
GAP W/O SUBSIDY	($506,548)
GAP FROM ABOVE	($506,548)
SECTION 8 / CHAPTER 707 INCOME	$65,527
GAP	($441,020)
GAP FROM ABOVE	($441,020)
TAX CREDIT INCOME	$0
GAP	($441,020)
EXISTING GAP FROM ABOVE	($441,020)
SHARP INCOME	$124,560
FINAL BEFORE TAX CASH FLOW	($316,460)
GAP REQUIRED TO BREAK EVEN	($316,460)
GAP INCLUDING A RETURN ON EQUITY OF 6.60%	$396,669

OPERATING PRO FORMA (YEAR 1, FIRST STABILIZED YEAR)

TOTAL INCOME AND SUBSIDIES:			
Market Rate Units:			
1 Bedroom	32	$750	$273,600
2 Bedroom	32	$1,000	$364,800
Moderate Income Units:			
2 Bedroom	12	$873	$125,748
3 Bedroom	6	$976	$70,254
Low Income Units:			
2 Bedroom	12	$907	$130,536
3 Bedroom	6	$1,123	$80,856
TOTAL INCOME AND SUBSIDIES)			$1,045,794

(See Income schedule for specific subsidy breakdowns)

EXPENSES:		
Operating Expenses	$1.50 /NSF	($277,687)
Real Estate Taxes	$0.95 /NSF	($75,372)
TOTAL EXPENSES:)		($353,059)
NET OPERATING INCOME:		$692,735
ANNUAL DEBT SERVICE:		($1,009,196)
Principal	$10,937,467	
Interest Rate	8.50%	
Term (Years)	30	
BEFORE TAX CASH FLOW (GAP))		($316,460)

PRO FORMA ANALYSIS   PHASE 1B   VACANT PARCELS #5 - 14
PARCEL DESCRIPTION: #5 C, 6A, 7A, 25-A, 4-12A, 4-12C, 33B.
PREPARED BY THE WESTERN REDEVELOPMENT AUTHORITY

DEVELOPMENT PROGRAM

PARCEL AREA	56,237 GSF
NUMBER OF UNITS	100 UNITS
PARKING SPACES	70 SPACES
EQUITY REQUIREMENT	10.00% OF TDC EQUITY

UNIT MIX:

MARKET RATE	50.0%	NO INCOME LIMIT
MODERATE INCOME	25.0%	UNIT MORE THAN 80% OF SMSA MEDIAN INCOME
LOW INCOME	25.0%	UNIT MORE THAN 50% OF SMSA MEDIAN INCOME

UNIT COMPOSITION	NO UNITS	% REF	GSF	NSF	EFFICIENCY
MARKET RATE UNITS					
1 BEDROOM UNITS	25	50%	700	595	85.0%
2 BEDROOM UNITS	25	50%	1,000	850	85.0%
TOTAL MARKET RATE UNITS	50	100%	42,500	36,125	85.0%
MODERATE INCOME					
2 BEDROOM UNITS	17	67%	1,000	850	85.0%
3 BEDROOM UNITS	8	33%	1,245	1,058	85.0%
TOTAL MODERATE RATE UNITS	25	100%	26,960	22,916	85.0%
LOW INCOME					
2 BEDROOM UNITS	17	67%	1,000	850	85.0%
3 BEDROOM UNITS	8	33%	1,245	1,058	85.0%
TOTAL LOW INCOME UNITS	25	100%	26,960	22,916	85.0%
TOTAL	100		96,420	81,957	

DEVELOPMENT PRO FORMA	UNIT COST	TOTAL COST
• LAND COST		
MARKET RATE UNITS	$25,000.00 /UNIT (FMV)	$1,250,000
MODERATE INCOME UNITS	$0.00 /UNIT (FMV)	$0
LOW INCOME UNITS	$0.00 /UNIT (FMV)	$0
TOTAL LAND COST		$1,250,000
HARD COSTS		
RESIDENTIAL CONSTRUCTION PER GSF	$90	$8,677,800
TOTAL HARD AND LAND COSTS		$9,927,800
PROJECT RELATED SOFT COSTS		
A/E FEE	4.0% OF HC	$347,112
LEGAL FEES	1.5% OF HC	$130,167
ACCOUNTING FEES	0.5% OF HC	$117,256
DEVELOPER'S FEE	4.0% OF HC	$347,112
RE TAXES DURING CONSTRUCTION		$46,414
INSURANCE, TITLE, PERMITS	1.0% OF HC	$86,778
RENT UP AND MARKETING (MARKET)	$600 /UNIT	$30,000
RENT UP AND MARKETING (LOW-MOD)	$300 /UNIT	$15,000
	10.0%	$464,522
CONSTRUCTION INTEREST @	10.0%	$504,979
TOTAL SOFT COSTS		$1,705,631
TOTAL PROJECT COSTS		$11,633,431
CONTINGENCY (% OF HARD COSTS)	5.0%	$433,890
TOTAL DEVELOPMENT COST		$12,067,321
EQUITY REQUIREMENT	10.0%	$1,206,752
TDC/GSF		$125.16
TDC/1 BEDROOM UNIT		$87,609
TDC/2 BEDROOM UNIT		$125,156
TDC/3 BEDROOM UNIT		$155,819

OPTION IIE

RENPCT=0
SEC 8=0
SMOD=0
SUB MOD=0
P-SM=0
P-LM=0
MKT=0
LI=0
INT RATE
MKT   8.5%
MOD   50.00%
LOW   25.00%
SIZE RATE   1.90%
INFLATER   3.00%

-08-

RENTAL INCOME SCHEDULE (YEAR 1, FIRST STABILIZED YEAR)

	Monthly Income/Unit	Yearly Income
TENANT INCOME:		
Market Rate Units:		
1 Bedroom	$750	$213,750
2 Bedrooms	$1,000	$285,000
Moderate Income Units:		
2 Bedrooms	$615	$123,463
3 Bedrooms	$625	$82,472
Low Income Units:		
2 Bedrooms	$397	$75,939
3 Bedrooms	$438	$63,638
TOTAL TENANT INCOME:		$800,257

SECTION 8/CHAPTER 707 SUBSIDY INCOME
Low Income:		
2 Bedroom	$273	$52,907
3 Bedroom	$312	$37,574
TOTAL SECTION 8/707 INCOME:		$90,482

SYNDICATION - TAX CREDIT (10 YEARS):
Low Income:		
2 Bedroom	$174	$35,514
3 Bedroom	$182	$17,492
TOTAL Syndication		$53,006

SHARP PROGRAM:
Moderate Income:		
2 Bedroom	$270	$55,080
3 Bedroom	$325	$31,200
Low Income:		
2 Bedroom	$270	$55,080
3 Bedroom	$325	$31,200
TOTAL SHARP INCOME:		$172,560

GAP ANALYSIS (YEAR 1)

ASSUMPTIONS:

OPTION
- RUMP (I-A)
- SEC 8-A
- SHARP(H-4)
- SUB-DND(H)
- P-SHIP(H)
- VACANCY
- NFA(I-I)
- Rate
- INFLATION FACTOR   1.5%
                       5.0%

OPERATING EXPENSES	($1,002,119)
DEBT SERVICE	($1,002,119)
TENANT INCOME	$800,257
GAP W/O SUBSIDY	($504,570)

GAP FROM ABOVE	($504,570)
SECTION 8 / CHAPTER 707 INCOME	$99,442
GAP	($475,085)

GAP FROM ABOVE	($475,085)
TAX CREDIT INCOME	$53,006
GAP	($422,083)

EXISTING GAP FROM ABOVE	($422,083)
SHARP INCOME	$172,560
FINAL BEFORE TAX CASH FLOW	($259,523)
GAP REQUIRED TO BREAK EVEN	($256,523)
GAP INCLUDING A RETURN ON EQUITY OF 6.0%	$339,168

OPERATING PRO FORMA (YEAR 1, FIRST STABILIZED YEAR)

TOTAL INCOME AND SUBSIDIES:

Market Rate Units		
1 Bedroom	$750	$213,750
2 Bedrooms	$1,000	$285,000
Moderate Income Units		
2 Bedrooms	$873	$178,543
3 Bedrooms	$916	$93,632
Low Income Units		
2 Bedrooms	$1,081	$220,340
3 Bedrooms	$1,205	$125,300
TOTAL INCOME AND SUBSIDIES		$1,116,305

(See income schedule for specific subsidy breakdown)

EXPENSES:

Operating Expenses	$1.50 /NSF	$826,650
Real Estate Taxes	$0.55 /NSF	$1,177,659
TOTAL EXPENSES		$736,709
NET OPERATING INCOME		$759.5%

ANNUAL DEBT SERVICE:
Principal $10,460,768
Interest Rate 5.00%
Term (Years) 30   ($4,000,119)

BEFORE TAX CASH FLOW (GAP)   ($259,523)

FIFTEEN YEAR OPERATING PRO FORMA

CALENDAR YEAR	1989	1990	1991	1992	1993	1994	1995	1996	1997	1998	1999	2000	2001	2002	2003	2004
PROJECT YEAR	1	2	3	4	5	6	7	8	9	10	11	12	13	14	15	16
INFLATION/YEAR 5.00%																

INCOME AND SUBSIDIES

TOTAL TENANT INCOME	800,257	840,270	882,284	926,398	972,718	1,021,354	1,072,421	1,126,042	1,182,344	1,241,462	1,303,535	1,368,711	1,437,147	1,509,004	1,584,455	1,663,677
TOTAL SECTION 8/CHAPTER 707 INCOME	94,482	95,006	99,756	104,744	109,981	115,480	121,254	127,317	133,683	140,367	147,385	154,755	162,492	170,617	179,148	188,105
TOTAL TAX SYNDICATION	53,006	53,006	53,006	53,006	53,006	53,006	53,006	53,006	53,006	53,006	0	0	0	0	0	0
TOTAL SHARP INCOME	172,560	163,932	155,735	147,949	140,551	133,524	126,847	120,505	114,480	108,756	103,318	98,152	93,707	48,095	33,666	0
TOTAL INCOME AND SUBSIDIES	1,116,305	1,152,214	1,190,781	1,232,096	1,276,256	1,323,363	1,373,529	1,426,870	1,483,513	1,543,590	1,554,238	1,621,618	1,668,346	1,727,716	1,797,268	1,851,782

EXPENSES

OPERATING EXPENSES 11.50%	696,694	801,192	816,552	832,664	849,627	866,101	884,681	903,569	923,070	944,998	967,208	990,610	1,013,100	1,049,830	1,067,902	1,096,909
REAL ESTATE TAXES 10.50%	177,879	181,752	185,840	190,132	194,630	199,390	194,329	107,263	112,633	120,783	126,824	133,163	139,834	146,805	154,356	161,641
TOTAL EXPENSES	884,709	882,944	102,091	1,022,196	1,043,366	1,065,471	1,088,741	1,113,183	1,530,841	565,783	1594,025	1623,775	1654,964	1687,710	1722,090	1758,203

South End
S727
1987

AUTHOR

SENHI

TITLE

DATE LOANED	BORROWER S NAME

CPSIA information can be obtained
at www.ICGtesting.com
Printed in the USA
BVHW070139150920
588713BV00001B/73